"Who's that knocking at my door?"

Barnacle Bill the Sailor and his Mates in Song and Story

OCCASIONAL PAPERS IN FOLKLORE
No. 5

SIMON J. BRONNER

"Who's that knocking at my door?"

Barnacle Bill the Sailor and his Mates in Song and Story

CAMSCO Music
1308 Brittany Pointe
Lansdale, PA 19446
800-548-FOLK

Loomis House Press
www.loomishousepress.com

ISBN 978-1-935243-83-0

Edited by Ed Cray (cray@usc.edu)

To Louis Peter Grijp (1954–2016), for bringing me over the sea

CONTENTS

LIST OF FIGURES

PREFACE AND ACKNOWLEDGMENTS

The tune and opening line of "Who's that knocking on my door?," from the song popularly known as "Barnacle Bill the Sailor," is hard to get out of my head.

Maybe you have the same response long after you first heard the song as a youth. I have vivid memories of him coming up in song at bawdy adolescent male gatherings, with, and without drink. The simple tune invited improvisation around a clear story line of a seaman's sexual bravado and it went on seemingly forever with different guys pitching in creative rhymed lyrics.

The song was also memorable because of its performance. Emboldened fellows bellowed with gusto the alternating voices of Bill and a young maiden. They delivered the maiden's question about the identity of the knocker in a dulcet falsetto and when taking the role of the sailor, answered in a gruff, bellicose growl. You did not have to be a great singer to chime in; the song compelled participation, and inevitably produced laughs and bonded the gathered group.

The scenario involved him coming on land in search of a sexual conquest after an extended period away at sea. The singers, usually adolescent boys, were not necessarily sailors but they related to this dominating get-whatever-he-wants character who was not about to let doors or decorum stop him. They could visualize him as big and burly, probably bearded, who stood out in his sailor outfit when he swaggered down the street. It was hard to escape popular culture references to it with toys, Halloween costumes, names of seafood restaurants, and occasional nostalgic reruns of him in Popeye and Betty Boop cartoons.

I could relegate Barnacle Bill to an irreverent youthful memory but into the twenty-first century he kept coming back into view. He arose when my basketball team celebrated a victory and I became aware of him again in classic movies and jazz recordings. In fieldwork in upstate New York for the *Archive of New York State Folklife*, I collected several examples but did not analyze them because I was preoccupied with the fiddle and dance tunes of northern old-time music (Bronner 1987).

As a professor of folklore, I heard students offer him up when pressed to think of folk singing. Since they imagined that old-time ballad singing was long moribund, they appeared surprised to realize that a living folk tradition of song and story was very much part of their lives. They related experiences in bars, fraternity houses, team outings, and adding to my curiosity, in sororities and all-woman sleepovers. As adviser to a military veterans' club, I also discovered that often more senior navy men and women engaged in singing the ditty along with other sailor songs at various dining events.

On sabbatical leave in England, and in correspondence with Australian colleagues, he came up again as I was introduced to "Bollicky Bill," a clear relation if not antecedent of old Barnacle. Looking through sheet music and broadsides at the Bodleian Library in Oxford, I learned of Bill's extended family of "Abram Brown," "Abel Brown," and "Rollicking Bill."

What I did not have is much scholarship to go on to assess Barnacle Bill's longevity and sources, and the meaning of his dialogues. I figured that his bawdiness contributed to scholarly aversion to his life story. Then in the same year G. Legman annotated Vance Randolph's "unprintable" risqué folksong collection (1992) and Ed Cray came out with *The Erotic Muse* (1992) that appeared to open broader inquiry into the rich tradition of bawdy songs. Truth is that Cray did not care much for Bill. He preferred others with more complex melodies and lyrics. I thought, though, that he missed the creative aspects of the song and certainly the folkloric contexts.

I did not immediately dive into unpacking Bill's many contexts, and first worked on the long bawdy adolescent recitations given by a single teller of Lady Lil also known as "Our [Eskimo] Nell" (Baker and Bronner 2005). I analyzed it as a masculine play "frame" for the free expression of attitudes that would receive opprobrium in the society in which singers participated. I viewed its performance more as an escape than a reflection of society and psychology suggested its significance for adolescent males who were forming their self-identity. While "Lady Lil" was not a dialogue song, the contexts in which Lil appeared were similar to Bill's and I resumed my query.

Omitted from most folksong indexes, variants of "Barnacle Bill" were assigned a number in the *Roud Folksong Index* (4704) and Robert Waltz's *Ballad Index* (EM081). With their coverage of texts in different English-speaking countries beginning in 1917, they were good databases for comparative work, both as folk songs and commercial recordings. Waltz indexed Bill under the title of "Bollochy Bill the Sailor" and I still had to reconcile the continuities and divergences between Barnacle and Bollochy Bill, and their Brown kin. Another issue was identifying the forms that traditions about Bill took. Waltz gave him credit as a ballad, but he was also anthologized as a "rugby song," "sea chantey," "sailor ditty," and a set of floating verses without a story line. I also found legends about memorable characters named Barnacle and Bollicky Bill that I wanted to compare with the songs to see if there was any connection. The investigation came together when I was invited to the fortieth International Ballad Conference in Amsterdam and Terschelling, The Netherlands, in 2010. I am not sure my audience fully appreciated Bill in the way that they revered classic characters from Child ballads such as "Lord Randall" and "Sir Patrick Spens," but colleagues were generous with suggestions.

Once having identified various types and contexts of songs and stories with sailor Bill in them, I tackled their meanings and wanted to explain the character's appeal for different ages and groups. My contention is that this material is ripe for symbolic analysis because it is in my estimation the most persistent narrative folk song invoking the seamen's image by sailor and landlubber alike. I hypothesize that rather than decreasing in popularity as a result of societal feminization, the song's reach has extended more widely.

"Barnacle Bill" as a modern narrative since industrialization and subsequently the cyber-age uses the sailor character to express a hyper-masculine fantasy in the context of polite society. The sailor character among manly heroes is an especially significant symbol, because it embodies, more than other brawny figures, with both feminine and masculine traits. Although having different sources in sailor occupational culture and street balladry, in various modern settings, or what I would call "play frames," the song exaggerates for coming-of-age men a legendary sailor's machismo and domestic responsibilities that might be called feminine.

Imagining themselves as "out to sea," young men relate to the song to bring into relief expectations of their proper behavior where they land.

The use of the character in story and song might be thought of as a psychological release, but its longevity in folk practices suggests more going on. In conjunction with one's "mates," it voices concerns for being out on one's own and the limits placed on individualism by romantic and other social connections.

Arriving at this thesis, I am grateful to the audiences to whom I made presentations on the subject. I was especially fortunate to have the ear of fellow folklorists who had conducted related work: Angus Gillespie, Jay Mechling, Ronald L. Baker, Jonathan Lighter, Revell Carr, Steve Roud, and Skip Taft. The research took me to repositories on both sides of the Atlantic, and I thank the following scholars and institutions for providing texts and supplementary material: Louis Grijp, Peter Jan Margry, and Martine de Bruin of the Meertens Institute in Amsterdam, the Netherlands; Bill Nicolaisen and Thomas McKean of the University of Aberdeen, Scotland; Daniel Wojcik at the University of Oregon's Randall V. Mills Archives of Northwest Folklore; Mary Ann Duncan at the Indiana State University's Folklore Archives; Warren Fahey of the Australian Folklore Unit; Graham McDonald at the National Film and Sound Archive in Australia; Alexa Hagerty of the University of California, Berkeley, Folklore Archive; Ann Hoog of the Archive of Folk Culture at the Library of Congress; and Jessica Suess of the Bodleian Library at the University of Oxford.

Special recognition and my dedication go out to Louis Grijp (1954–2016) who first approached me during my fellowship stay at the Meertens Institute about developing this topic. He passed away way too soon, but in his short time with us, he left a tremendous legacy of folk musical research sure to inspire future work.

PONDERING BOLLICKY SAILORS

It's quite possible that most ballad scholars are landlubbers. They seem not to have thought of seafarers' songs in the lot of romantic, heroic, and tragic ballads dominating folk song anthologies. A look at the index of W. Edson Richmond's *Ballad Scholarship: An Annotated Bibliography* (1989) provides relevant evidence of the latter tendency. Much as I admired Richmond as scholar and teacher deep inland at Indiana University where I completed my doctoral work, I noticed that after 287 pages of entries covering articles and books from around the world, he did not even list "sea" or "sailor" in the index. Yet well he might, since ballads on the disguised or returning lover theme, sometimes called the most popular collected romantic ballad, typically feature a sailor as the absent male (Rennick 1959). One could also point to Malcolm Laws's codification of 28 *Ballads of Sailors and the Sea* (section D) as genuine native American ballads (1964: 161–74). Nonetheless, it is true, as D.K. Wilgus points out in his historiographical *Anglo-American Folksong Scholarship since 1898* (1959) that scholarly attention to sailors' songs came late compared to other musical traditions: work chanteys start showing up in collections in the 1830s, but a ballad repertory is not separately analyzed until the twentieth century (217; for chronicles of earlier chanteying, see Broadwood 1928; Saunders 1928).

Notable in putting together maritime ballads in one English volume is antiquarian James Orchard Halliwell's *Naval Ballads of England* (1841) for the Percy Society, in which he complained that Britain's "triumphs of our marine power cannot be too frequently recalled to our memories." He hoped that the volume would change "the directions of the thoughts so induced" (viii). He offered isolated examples to show a long lineage of ballads of the sea such as his earliest texts hailing from the fifteenth century. He was aware, too, of the whaling ballad "Voyage to Greenland" included in *A Collection of Old Ballads* (1725), but noted that the rich repertoire of naval ballads was being missed by most antiquarians even in a maritime nation such as Britain. Sailors' folk singing and broadsides were often out of sight and therefore out of mind.

Whether as a function of nationalism in folkloric collection with its equation of country or region to the boundaries of the "land," connection to the news, and broadsides, of the street; a domestic, often feminized context for ballad content; or an avoidance of bawdy content associated with sailors, scholars have tended to associate ballads with terra firma.

Historically, John Lomax had a profound impact in *Cowboy Songs and Other Frontier Ballads* (1910) and *Songs of the Cattle Trail and Cow Camp* (1919) on British-American ballad scholarship. Lomax suggested a relationship of folk musical production to the presence of a frontier or border region, a theme picked up across the ocean in David Buchan's *The Ballad and The Folk* (1972). As more became known about sailor ballads, the perception from sailors became apparent of land being in symbolic relation to water as tame is to wild. This viewpoint has a bearing on my analysis of a sexually tinged narrative in sailor ballads of the "vast, deep sea."

My query has a precedent in comparative folkloric work of the nineteenth century, apparently made in response to the scholarly priority given to landed narrative and belief. Most notably, the title of Laura Alexandrine Smith's *Music of the Waters* (1888) suggests a study of the symbolism of water and land in ballad and song. Although mentioning the inspiration of the ocean to "our literature of the sea," the volume contains no separate categorization of sea balladry. Instead, it characterizes sailors' musical expressiveness as utilitarian work songs and clever brief "ditties."

Smith was aware of usually pejorative lyrics *about* sailors on shore, but the news of her book was its presentation of songs *by* sailors. With its attention to songs of maritime nations drawn primarily from sailors themselves, it made a claim to be "original in its conception and execution" (ix). Devoted mostly to identifying rather than interpreting songs, it nonetheless made an appeal to scholars to investigate sailors' material as worthy of serious study. It should have egged on researchers with its suggestion of a psychic unity among sailors globally. Smith's book broadened the usual scope of water in song beyond ocean-bound sailors with references to fishermen, boatmen, and rowing songs, superstitions, and legends. Smith observed that from the usual musical vantage of the shore, songs of watermen appear to have no meaning, and are distinctive to the countries that produce them rather than possessing a thematic or psychological connection. Yet she wonders why sailors, in addition to using songs for work, "will as soon listen to a ballad as a yarn..." which requires what the hearer of old ballads demanded, "plenty of stirring incident and strong true feeling simply expressed" (xxv). Her answer involved the general appeal of ballad on sea and shore as entertainment. Taking this conflict one step further, one can observe that the songs ocean-going sailors sang in response to more risk out on the "raging sea" entailed more references to ghosts and taboos than those of fisher and boat men closer to shore (see Mullen 1969; Poggie, Pollnac, and Gersuny 1976).

Heroic ballads and beliefs involving sailors and the sea have attracted historical comment, including Thomas Percy's inclusion of "Sir Patrick Spens" in his *Reliques of Ancient English Poetry* (1765) with the lines that "Sir Patrick Spens is the best sailor, That sails upon the se" (62). Yet Percy and later Francis James Child and Svend Grundtvig did not thematize such songs around their rhetorical use of the sea.

Perhaps one reason is that they did not consider the sea ballad corpus extensive or old enough to merit separate treatment. Alan Lomax in his oft-printed *The Folk Songs of North America* (1960) separated a category of classic "Old Ballads" from one for "Yankee Soldiers and Sailors," implying that songs of the sea were regionally delimited occupational songs of recent vintage. Even having segregated sailors' songs from the classic ballads, he was still open to the aesthetic or effete criticism of presenting songs by unsavory characters such as seafarers, miners, and woodsmen who at best produced "low" or "coarse" ballads; D.K. Wilgus summarizes these as unusual, at least from a historiographical viewpoint, as "out-of-doors, physical endeavor" (1959:217). Thus ballad editors categorized seamen's material under songs of romance or war rather than occupation or water. Sophie Jewett in *Folk-Ballads of Southern Europe* (1913), for instance, included the Catalan ballad "The Sailor" in her anthology as an example of "ballads of love" rather than songs of the sea.

Besides romance, war turned heads toward folk-eyed views of conflict and danger, since chanteys were more commonly associated with merchant service than warships. A number of chronicles of battles merit inclusion in Laws's category of sea ballads, and sailors' ballads peppered books on songs of soldiers appearing after World War I (Bennett 2000; Brophy and Partridge 1965; Henderson 1947; Hopkins 1978). This inclusion was notable because previously, in the age of sail, when sailors were profiled for their music it was for work "shanties" (from the "shanty" on board) or "chanteys" (suggesting that they were more formulaic chants than narrative songs).

A raft of mid-nineteenth century writers adapted airs coming out of the mouths of sailors and published lyrics, usually with the commentary that one hardly expected creative, even artistic, verse emanating from seamen who were considered of low status occupationally and of low reputation morally. The reports on seafaring traditions in the wake of industrialization were often meant to lament the passing of a golden age of sail with the further implication that sailors sang no more. For instance, John Ashton in his compendium of 1891, *Real Sailor-Songs* flatly declared that "The day of Real Sailor-Songs has long since passed and gone" (1). What remained of sailors' ballads, he observed, came out of music halls. He explained the supposed demise of the songs by the breakdown of seamen's isolation and consequently their folk culture. He wrote, "Except in the Navy, there are no long cruises, and the short voyages enable seafarers to keep themselves *au courant* with the last thing out in Songs" (1). He waxed nostalgic for the "old ones," which he called the epic "Chants of Roland." Ballads of thirty or forty verses, "having been handed down from generation to generation," he pointed out, were signs of their antiquity. Songs of three to six verses to him were clearly "modern" (1). Further lending the old ballads authenticity, he felt, was the fact that "They were odorous of the Sea, because they were of it, and were part and parcel of the life thereon" (1). He tried to show in his compilation that sailors' songs were about more than work. Whether sung in "Forecastle" (work) or "Ward-room" (play), they showed, he claimed, "poetic genius."

Acceptance of sailors' material as artistic was not an easy sell. Charles Didbin (1745–1814), for example, countered disdain for sailors as vulgar by composing new, apparently unoffensive sea songs. There are hints of his folk sources in *Sea Songs and Ballads* (1823) which he dedicated to "the Sailors of Britain," whose balladry, in the past, he wrote, "records their generosity and fearlessness, and celebrates many of their glories" (v).

His work directly inspired the likes of poet Ned Halyard in *Sea Songs, Tales, Etc.* (1849) who composed sentimental songs paying homage to the sailors and their mothers, but still warned that they might offend women and married men (vii). In 1841, James Orchard Halliwell admitted to readers that his collection of early naval ballads was incomplete because he "found it necessary to omit a few ballads of the sea, which might have been introduced, owing to their occasional grossness" (viii).

Despite Ashton's eulogy for sailors' folk songs, ballads kept cropping up in late-nineteenth century musical collections from oral tradition. Yet the collectors trivialized the seamen's songs as "ditties," demonstrating rhyming formulas and social devices for work routines rather than artistic, lyrical narratives. Reflecting this perspective on sailor songs, collectors such as Elizabeth Bristol Greenleaf and Grace Yarrow Mansfield in their *Ballads and Sea-Songs of Newfoundland* (1933) separated heroic ballads from songs of the sea. If they did not incorporate sailor songs into the ballad tradition established by literary scholars, they nonetheless contemplated the sea as theme in song. They reflected that the isolated life on the sea and recognition of the dangers in fishing and seafaring led to a fair share of commentary in song. Explaining the often unexpected role of gruff sailors as singers, Greenleaf and Yarrow characterized sailing as tough intensive work interspersed with often long periods of doldrums. Song presumably lightened the dull hours or eased the work of hauling and heaving on frequently undermanned merchant ships.

Beyond this pragmatic interpretation, Smith in *Music of the Waters* hinted at some psychological analysis when she stated that sailor chanties are "the true expression of the feelings of the men who originate them—the strangest men perhaps, taking them all in, one can meet with" (1888:xxii). Mentioning the terrible conditions of the seafaring life, she wrote that "we must confess a sailor's life has much to make it undesirable, and yet, for all that, taking them as a class, they are healthy, hearty fellows, and well deserving of the epithet of 'Jolly Tars'" (xxiii). One could hypothesize from that statement a function of song as emotional release or escape in addition to work utility, and I will expand on that proposition shortly, in social psychological context rather than, as she claimed, a result of an innate psychic unity.

One of the few comparative references in English to the theme of the sea in balladry is provided by Countess Evelyn Martinengo-Cesaresco in *Essays in the Study of Folk-Songs* (1886), although she sounds dismissive of much creative inspiration coming from the sea. "Sea-views of the sea, rare in poetry of any sort," she wrote, "can scarcely be said to exist in folk-poesy." She probably was speaking as a member of the landed gentry without the benefit of collections on the waters. She observed, for example, that "sailors' songs have generally not much to do with the wonders of the deep; the larger body of them are known to be picked up on land, and the few exceptions to the rule are mostly kept from the ken of the outer and profane public. The Basque sailors have certain songs of their own, but only a solitary fragment of one of them has ever been set on record. Once when a Basque was asked to repeat a song he had been heard singing, he quietly said that he only taught it to those who sailed with him."

The fragment just mentioned speaks of the silver trumpet (the master's whistle?) sounding over the waters at break of day, while the coast of Holland shimmers in the distance. "The first glimpse of a level reach of land in the morning haze could hardly be better described" (37). The sea, she generalized, is viewed abstractly or incidentally by its depth and vastness, but she does not expand on the possible psychological response in what she calls the "frequent recurrence of phrases such as 'the waters of the sea are vast, you cannot discern the bottom' (Basque); 'High is the starry sky, profound the abyss of ocean' (Russian)" (37–38).

One could ponder the favor for songs "picked up on land" about seamen. A number of collections note with little comment that sailors and the sea show up in songs deep inland performed by farming families contemporaneously with the age of sail (see Harold Thompson, 1958: 49–53; Flanders and Brown 1931:141–47). Well past this era into the twenty-first century, songs about sailors pepper bawdy singing performances at fraternity parties, rugby celebrations, bachelor parties, and drinking bashes. Thus two problems are posed in the categorization of "sea songs and ballads." One is the representation of the sailor and sea as subject and the other is the role taken by the sailor as performer. The common approach to these issues is to contextualize the texts and situations in which the practice of song is evident.

In the introduction to *The Ballad and the Scholars: Approaches to Ballad Study* (1986), Wayland Hand writes that "each approach needs the other" (xi). They are both aligned in their attention to the interpretation of songs' function in society and the role of the singer set in a cultural context or compared across cultures. I voice general agreement with his principled declaration, but want to suggest that such approaches often stop short of symbolic analysis that gets at cognitive sources to explain the production of culture and the persistence of tradition. Such a symbolic analysis often comes out of attention to cultural practice as context and rhetorical readings of communicated texts.

I want to demonstrate in this essay a thematic query with a look at the symbolism of sailor and sea in song with particular reference to a complex of songs revolving around the figure of "Abram Brown," "Abel Brown," "Bollicky Bill," "Rollicking Bill," or most popularly "Barnacle Bill" (as indexed in the Roud Folk Song Index as 4704). I choose this material for symbolic analysis because it may be the most persistent narrative folk song invoking the seamen's image by sailor and landlubber alike and therefore raises questions about its appeal over time. It also sets up a thematic interpretation of the distinctiveness of the open waters because of its memorable first line "It's just me from over the sea" (and the variants "I am home from over the sea" and "It's I myself and nobody else") that resounds in other sailor songs. Although the song is so pervasive in English-speaking nations, it has escaped analysis, probably because of its bawdy content. Or else it has been dismissed for a supposed lack of artistry. Ed Cray, for example, editorializes that "this song, unlike so many folk songs, has little to recommend it. Its melody is monotonous; its lyrics are repetitious to the point of idiocy" (1992: 81). Cray misses its creative appeal, however, as a narrative as well as linguistic structure allowing for individual and communal improvisation, often in the performative context of a male drinking session that leads to song.

Another bias in folk musical scholarship concerns the song's antiquity and folk authenticity; scholars belittle it as a "low ballad" or "drinking song" influenced by popular recordings and broadcasts, apparently of recent origin, rather than examining it historically as a broadside ballad, folk ballad parody, or ballad-like piece. I claim that its importance is based, if not on aesthetic grounds, on the "symbolic capital" relating to the image of the sailor and the deep, vast sea it provides and on its continued global popularity over the course of three centuries.

My selection of variants of "Barnacle Bill" as representative is therefore different from the analytical strategy of folklorist Alan Dundes who turned his psychoanalytic lens on the ballad of "The Walled-Up Wife" because of the vast amount of scholarship devoted to it. Dundes concentrated on the symbolism of the man's erection of buildings rather than the water in which the builder's wife is tragically immersed. Looking for more explanation for the ballad's persistence than its entertainment value, he wanted to raise the possibility of metaphorical meanings for narratives that cut across the categories from different countries or lands. His thesis was that in the ballad the castle, bridge, or well-structures all involve or encase water—"men force a sacrificial woman to be enclosed in a man-made construction—just as men were originally enclosed in a female womb" (2007: 120). His analysis of the ballad expanded on work he did elsewhere concerning wishing wells, sailor jokes, and flood myths suggesting a maternal symbolism of water projected in folklore (see

Dundes 2007), which I test further with masculine performances of "Barnacle Bill." I draw on early texts from oral tradition from the Robert Gordon Collection in the Library of Congress that had been previously suppressed in a supposedly obscene "inferno" file. Other unpublished sources I mine are folk song collector Sam Eskin's set of private notebooks from the mid-twentieth century that he labeled "delta" to mark bawdy content and several caches of material in university folklore archives. To provide context for these texts, I interviewed veteran sailors and was able to ethnographically record events in which "Barnacle Bill" was spontaneously performed, including "dining-in" naval events.

A question raised by such rowdy events is whether the performative frame with its symbolic metacommunication about water contains similar messages for men—and in some cases women—on land as well as on ship. Pursuing this question compels me to apply a structuralist apparatus that Roger Renwick argues should allow ballad analysts "to see more clearly not just *what* a meaning might be but also *how* that meaning is articulated" (1985: 406).

My goal is to do more than an alternative reading of texts, even if in context, but to locate, in Renwick's words, "*relationships* among parts, even *relationships among relationships*" (1985: 406). A conspicuous example of relationships I expose here is of sexual choices of marital commitment, considered feminized, or philandering activity associated with manliness.

TEXTS, TYPES, AND RELATIONSHIPS

The texts of "Barnacle Bill" are hardly subtle with their references first to gender differences and then to sexual attributes. Structured as a dialogue with characters identified in the third person, the song inevitably opens with the femininely asked question "Who's that knocking at my door?" and the introduction of the voice as that of "the fair young maiden." The response, usually performed in a low, throaty, quickly paced manner is "It's me from over the sea." The opposition between ship and shore is set as one that is masculine and passively feminine, respectively. If the maiden is demure, sober, and obedient to parents and the rules of society, Bill is drunk, crude, and defiant. He comes from far away and apparently has been at sea a long time. She may ask him what he wants to do, such as the frequently used line, "Do you want to go to a dance?" to which Bill responds, "To hell with the dance, I'll pull (or you pull) down my (your) pants." He may announce that he is home after being at sea for years, or state directly his desire for sex with the line "I just got paid and I want to get laid" or "It's me and my crew and we've come for a screw!" In most versions, the maiden hesitates to open the door, and Bill becomes agitated and physically aggressive, often threatening to knock down the door and any barriers she mentions. To the suggestion that she not let him in, he might disrespectfully reply, "Open the door and lie on the floor!" (or "be a whore") She might ask, "What if I should lock the door?" He typically answers back with the boast, "I'll smash the lock with my diamond-hard cock!"

I discern from the texts available four types of narrative formulas after the fairly standard opening. In the first type with a familiar romantic ballad theme, the apparently sheltered maiden rushes to open the door and welcomes his seduction in exchange for his promise of marriage. In the second type with a seduction argument, she tries to discourage him with the risks or obstacles in the way, such as having only a small bed or parents coming, but he will not refrain from his advances. In the third type, she lets him in for sex but uses metaphors to hide the successively more intimate acts (cf. the children's joke "Mommy, can I shower with you?" Bronner 1988: 136–37; Zumwalt 1976). Various answers may be supplied to the maiden's warning that her parents will discover them. In most versions, Bill kills the father and rapes the mother, although in some oral versions I have collected he has sex with both of them ("fuck the ma and suck the pa"), indicating his prowess at both hetero- and homosexuality.

The ending, if performed as a narrative rather than an improvisational formula, is about a pregnancy that results from intercourse with the maiden as daughter of parents who still live in the home. In the case of the first type, Bill reneges on his promise to marry. Addressing gender, the maiden asks what Bill will do if the child is a boy or a girl. In most cases, he unabashedly declares he will kill the girl and drive the boy to sea. As a result of being at sea, he implies, the boy will be just as morally corrupt and socially contrary as Barnacle Bill.

The maiden's part in the narrative is similar to bawdy versions of another sailor song, "Bell Bottom Trousers" (Hoffmann motif X724.8.3), probably hailing from the nineteenth century, with the chorus: "Singing Bell Bottom Trousers, Coats of Navy blue / He can climb the riggin' like his father used to do." The female narrator laments, "And I like a silly girl, thinking it no harm, I jumped into the sailor's bed, to keep the sailor warm" (Cray 1992: 72–78). The next day, the sailor is gone and he has a left a note stating, "If you have a daughter, take her on your knee / If you have a son, send the bastard out to sea."

A similar message given in the maiden's voice is expressed in "A Sailor is a Sailor," another song with the theme of pregnancy following a seduction by a sailor. It merits mention in the motive relationships with "Barnacle Bill" because of its announcement of the symbolic certainty of the sailor as a hypersexed character. The chorus is "For a sailor is a sailor wherever he may be / Now listen and I'll tell you what this sailor did to me" (Lynn 1963: 22). The "good girl" in the song walks past a sailor and he trails her home. He follows her, incrementally, up the stairs, as she turns out the light, and as she jumps into bed, all as she sings, "like a good girl should." The song concludes with "Nine months later, much to my surprise, I had a little boy with navy blue eyes, For a sailor is a sailor wherever he may be. And now I have told you what this sailor did to me."

Ed Cray speculates on a relation of the opening rhyming couplets of "Bollochy Bill" with "Snapoo," also associated with sailors in the nineteenth century, because of their aggressive sexuality: "So that son of a bitch, he took her to bed, And crammed it in from its roots to its head" (Cray 1992: 383). A further thematic connection is in the unwanted pregnancy and resulting child who continues his father's rowdy ways:

Oh, six months came, and six months past,
The rim of her belly hung down to her ass.

Oh, nine months came, and nine months past,
And a jolly young sailor rolled out of her ass. (Cray 1992: 382)

By the time of the birth in "Snapoo," the sailor is long gone and feels no responsibility for the child. In "Bollochy Bill the Sailor," Bill tells the maiden that he will see her no more after their sexual encounter. In longer versions, the maiden may ask what Bill will do if he is brought to justice for his crimes. As a brash, extraordinarily strong bad man, Bill is defiant and brags that no jail can hold him; he can "smash down the walls with my forty-pound balls!" or some other dramatic demonstration of his transgressive power such as "I'll lay a fart and blow it apart!" (an anal-erotic display of power also featured in adolescent male recitations such as "Lady Lil" or "Eskimo Nell" (see Baker and Bronner 2005).

The resulting child is also significant because of the frequent legacy of seafaring occupations running in family lines; as a result, psychological profiles of sailors often deal with an absent father and a dominant mother role in the boy's life before he goes off to sea (Burton and Whiting 1961; Grønseth and Tiller 1957). Thus sailors singing about an absent, apparently uncaring father may underlie the repeated theme of the father's attitude toward the child and the fate of the boy to become a sailor.

Folklore archives from the late twentieth century include a fourth type of Barnacle Bill narrative often contributed by women, perhaps indicative of a modern feminist twist. In this later type, the maiden is at first afraid of the sex. She demurs. Bill demands, but after giving in she finds she likes it and wants more from Bill. By the end of the song, she wears out Bill and ends up dominant (cf. the incrementally more sexual responses of the coy "Maid of Amsterdam" who turns out to be more experienced than she lets on to the sailor). Sometimes the text of the fourth type announces that a transformation occurs in her from fair young maiden to "Barnacle Bess the nympho" (i.e., nymphomaniac). This type has a narrative that turns the seduction into a fornication contest, reminiscent of recitations about a schoolmarm turned hypersexed powerhouse usually named Lil or Nell (see Baker and Bronner 2005). The name of Bess, besides forming an alliteration, also has a connection to life on the sea because of the association in popular nineteenth-century drama and song to a sailor's bride or lover (Frank 2010: 402–3).

Despite the identification in 1920 by *Time* magazine of "Rollicky Bill the Sailor" as an Elizabethan ballad, reference works tend to rely on the view of lexicographer Eric Partridge that the song "Ballocky Bill the Sailor" can be traced to Great Britain in the late nineteenth century ("Cinema" 1920; Partridge 1970: 29). He defines the character in his slang dictionary as a "mythical person commemorated in a late C. 19–20 low ballad and often mentioned, by way of evasion (cf. *Up in Annie's Room*), by the soldiers in the G.W. [Great War]. Bill is reputed to have been most generously testicled" (1970: 29). Being testicled, he was presumably hypermasculine in size as well as sexuality because the testes constitute the male generative gland of sperm as well as the testosterone hormone. Bill's large testicles contribute to an image of him as large, wide, and swaggering, even though he may be on the clumsy side. The allusions to "bollocky" or "ballsy" suggested an insolent, bold, and even reckless character.

Bill's physicality connotes a lack of intellectualism. He acts with brawn rather than brains. His endowment of testes also conveys sexual prowess, as expressed in the bawdy sailor song, "Every Ship Has a Capstan":

> Every ship has a capstan, has a capstan, has a capstan
> Every good ship has a capstan and a capstan has pawls
> And every young girl likes a young man
> With a big pair of balls. (Cray 1992: 60)

An additional characteristic associated with "bollocks" is uninhibited physical and verbal aggressiveness drawn from the free-swinging image of hanging testicles unrestrained by close-fitting briefs. The traditional clothing of seamen suitable for their work may have influenced this image, because in both British and American navies, sailor dress frequently included loose-fitting trousers with belts made of rope. (I should note that the bawdy song "Do Your Balls Hang Low?" reported widely in North America, Britain, and Australia is often sung to the tune of "Sailor's Hornpipe" with the chorus, "Do your balls hang low? / Do they swing to an' fro? / Can you tie 'em in a knot? / Can you tie 'em in a bow" [Cray 1992: 336–38].

Related to this reference of "coming undone" is Allen Walker Read's note on British slang of the verb "bollucking:" a loud, reprimanding tone shouted by commanding officers to the troops (1949: 154); and a superior who is especially demanding and therefore emasculating may be called a "ball-buster."

Perhaps less obvious but relevant in performances of the song is the implication that by being ballocky, Bill is an older, irascible sailor and experienced in the world because his testicles presumably hang lower and his girth is larger than a young slender, jolly "tar." If others mistake his maturity for a lack of vitality, he shows both his toughness and virility with sexual and alcoholic bravado. Although calling someone "bollocky" implies that his behavior is socially inappropriate or even deviant (see Pyles 1949: 4). In Australia, Bill is often "bullocky," referring to the driver of a bullock team who had reputations for being foul-mouthed and tough.

Musicologist James Fuld includes "Barnacle Bill the Sailor" in his *Book of World-Famous Music* (1985) and considers it to be a "relatively 'recent' folk song" (128). Yet he connects the narrative of the song to the tradition of the "night-visitor," which he calls "an old one in folk ballads, having been traced back to 1578" (129; see also Gilchrist 1924b). He gives as examples, without making a direct link, verses adapted from oral tradition by Robert Burns, notably "Wha is That at My Bower Door?" (1792). The text is also rendered in dialogue with the comparable opening,

> "Who is that at my bower door?"
> "O who is it but Findlay!"
> "Then go your way, you should not be here."
> "What makes you, so like a thief?"
> "O, come and see!" said Findlay.
> "Before the morning you will mischief?"
> "Indeed will I" said Findlay (translation).

According to James Johnson in the *Scots Musical Museum* (1787–1803), Burns based his lines on oral versions he heard and was inspired by the song "The Auld Man's Best Argument" in Allan Ramsay's *Tea-Table Miscellany: Or, A Collection of Choice Sangs* (1724), including "Widow, Are Ye Waking?" which begins

> "O Wha's that at my chamber door?"
> "Fair widow, are ye wawkin?"
> Auld carl, your suit give o'er,
> Your love lies a' in tawking. (Johnson and Stenhouse 1853: 317–18)

The last two lines translate into modern English as "Old man, give up your suit (wooing), Your love is all talk (rhyming with waking)." Oral versions have been collected in the nineteenth century as "The Wooer Came to the Widow's Door," such as the following from Andrew Crawford's fieldwork in the years 1826–28; it contains a progression from the door to the bed similar to "Barnacle Bill":

> The wooer cam to the widow's dore
> And fain wa he
> The wooer came to the widow's dore
> And fain was he I's warran
>
> Wooer, wooer, would ye be in
> O aye quo he quo he I's warran
> She opened and let him in
> And fain was he I's warran
>
> So wooer wooer wad ye hae a seat
> O aye quo he quo he I's warran
> She gied him a seat and he sat down
> And fain was he I's warran
>
> It's wooar wooar wad ye hae meat
> O aye quo he quo he I's warran
> She gied him bred and cheese to eat
> And fain and fain was he I's warran
>
> Sae wooar wooar wad ye hae a bed
> O aye quo he quo he I's warran
> She gied him a bed and he lay doun
> And fain and fain was he I's warran
>
> She jmpit behind him on the wa
> And squeek cryed he I's warran
> So woor woor waddye be out
> O aye quo he quo he I's warran
>
> She openit the dore and let him out
> And fain was he I's warran
> There being a hole afore the dore
> In fell he I's warran
>
> Woor woor I doubt ye are faun
> O aye quo he quo he I's warran
> Deil may care if ye cum out
> Amen cryed he cryed he I's warran.
>   (Lyle 1975: 188–89; see also Shoolbraid 2010: 106–8, 137; Spring 1988: 475–76)

The singer, John Smith, was not a sailor but a tailor; the collector intimated that the song came out of Smith's experience with his male cronies at the pub because the singer was, according to the collector's description, a "very thirsty man" (Spring 1988: 480). Smith's "A Wooer Came to the Widow's Door" also appears in the field collection of the Folk Song Society on the Isle of Man in the early twentieth century with the suggestive dialogue, "Hi, ho, will you be on? I mean," said he, / "Ho, ho," said she, / "Hi ho, will you be on? I mean," said she, / "I'm a true young man" (Gilchrist and Broadwood 1924: 136–37; see also Spring 1988: 476). The suitor in this set of songs hanging about the widow's door is young compared to Bollocky Bill, who is usually portrayed as older and unattractive; nonetheless, the possibility exists of a textual adaptation as an older sailor's song.

G. Legman more assertively than Fuld connects the Burns verse to "Bollocky Bill" by stating that the folksong on which "Wha is that at my bower door" is based "continues in the living tradition, in the burlesque "Bollocky Bill the Sailor" (1964: 201; see also Spring 1988: 481). He makes the jump from "Bollocky" representing abundant testicles to what he calls the "effete expurgation" of Barnacle Bill and finally to the mass cultural "Popeye the Sailor Man" (and his relationship to the coy Olive Oyl, and his rival Bluto who fits the crude Barnacle Bill image) (1964: 202). [He left out an intermediate step on the way to Popeye with Everett E. Lowry's popular newspaper comic-strips, "Binnacle Jim" from 1903 to 1909.]

According to the Dutch comiclopedia, the name was inspired by "Barnacle Bill," the leading character of an older series of particularly bawdy English sea ballads. (Lambiek 2010). They bear an uncanny resemblance to Popeye's graphic look. Lowry's earlier sailor Jim is muscular, bearded, bald, and appears older. He is a prankster, often tormenting the more rotund shipmate Bill Bunk; also drawing on folklore, he has a pet monkey with the legendary name of Davy Jones.

Legman finds the night-visit theme with dialogue between the brutal lover angrily mocking the genteel singing girl common in several countries, and draws comparisons to a Polish text of "Rozmowa Milosna" (translated into French as "Entretien amoureux," or Lovers' Conversation) and the Serbian "Poskochnika" in *Kryptádia* (1898, 233–34 for Polish, and 259–60 for French translation; for the Serbian text, 1884, 284–88).

Legman also could have mentioned the Dutch broadside ballad "Koddige t'Zamenspraek" (1718) that opens with the line "Wie komt er kloppen al aan mijn deur? (Who is knocking on my door?) (Meertens Instituut 2010). In that text, the knocker is a young man who expresses his regrets to a Franciscan priest that in the order he will not be able to drink, smoke, and play cards. The priest's reply insists that he marry a pretty maiden, with the implication that he cannot deny himself sexual pleasures.

The motif of knocking may suggest gesture, costuming, or dance accompanying the words, as occurs in the *Kryptádia* texts or other dramatized comic dialogues such as "Soldier, Soldier, Will You Marry Me?" and "The Quaker's Courtship" (Newell 1883: 93–95). A dance-rhyme collected in the field with a close resemblance to the "It's I myself" line in "Barnacle Bill" is identified by Annie Gilchrist as "A Pair of White Gloves," to the dance-tune "The Hempdresser," on the Isle of Man. Set in dialogue form, the lyrics open with the maiden's voice:

> "Oh, who is this that is at my door,
> That is knocking there so boldly?"
> "Is it not myself that is in? Said Abram Juan
> "And a pair of white gloves."   (Gilchrist 1924a: 173–74)

One might even speculate on the identity of "Abram Juan" as a variant (or wrong transcription) of Abram Brown, linking it to the song "Abram Brown the Sailor." Across the ocean in Texas, folklorist Roger Abrahams recorded potentially related jump rope rhymes that he identified as "echoes of 'Barnacle Bill the Sailor'":

> Who is knocking at my door?
> "It is I,"
> Said the fly,
> 1, 2, 3, 4.   (Abrahams 1963: 213)

What appears significant about the "It is I [or me]" line is the audacity with which it is performed. Gilchrist notes in her early fieldwork the performative emphasis on differentiating the "two voices by change of rhythm, tempo, or even key; the man's part being drawling and the woman's brisk" (Gilchrist and Broadwood 1924: 137). Not highly regarded or even feared by the female questioner, the knocker as a pestilent male appears intrusive; he does not belong inside—the maiden, house, or society. He is rhetorically set on the outside. In the sexual terms of "Barnacle Bill" he is knocking on the door before "knocking up" the maiden.

The frequent connection made in annotations of "Barnacle Bill" to the night-visitor theme of a male suitor unexpectedly or secretly entering his lady's chamber under the cloak of darkness raises the question of whether this observation suggests that Barnacle Bill is an historical outgrowth of previous night-visitor songs. (These are often traced to the category of 11th–12th century *aube* or *aubade* lament songs for lovers parting at dawn, primarily in the German, French, and British traditions.)

There is also a psychological commentary on the appeal of the songs' narrative, even if the performers or performances of the songs are not genetically or geographically linked.

Folklorist Barre Toelken finds possible historical contexts linking the songs in northern Europe with shared customs of knights or soldiers (he does not mention sailors!) expecting a night of love before going off to war, and assumptions about the natural cycle in which death and fertility are reciprocally associated. Nonetheless the song's typical sexual metaphors in different local contexts performed in modern settings are distinct from its historical ritual roots (Toelken 1995: 59–68; see also Baskerville 1921; Cattermole-Tally 1987–88).

If "Barnacle Bill" is related to historical night-visit songs, the lyrical relationships to imminent death and quiet dawn departure are absent. Toelken summarizes the main elements of the night-visit song as (1) the arrival of the lover, often guided or precipitated by an invitation from the young woman; (2) his entry into her house, chamber, or bower; (3) a reference to a cock crowing a warning of impending dawn (sometimes in the German versions the cock is replaced by a watchman); and (4) the retreat of the lover, usually without being detected by the girl's family (Toelken 1995: 63).

The opening often contains an ambiguity about the familiarity of the suitor to the lady. Toelken suggests that most night-visit songs are predicated on the intimacy of the young couple, although the parents probably disapprove of their tryst. In "Barnacle Bill," the lady treats the sailor as an intruder but appears in some versions interested in the seduction. This dramatic tension links "Barnacle Bill" to a subtype of night-visit songs identified by Charles Read Baskervill as "Open the door" narratives beginning with songs as early as 1586 (Baskervill 1921: 571). Baskervill summarizes the type as a lover's parley. "Conventionally," he wrote, "she makes a show of reluctance and finally yields, at times with an enlightening disregard of modern standards. The warning that the father and mother or some other member of the family will be awakened and will interfere is usual" (Baskervill 1921: 571).

The "Open the door" line likely became associated over time with sexual intrigue in the face of societal or parental repression. Baskervill comments that "these conventions of the night visit, though simple and natural enough in themselves, recur so persistently in different types of popular poetry as to suggest that to the popular mind the theme called for the use of certain formulas, and that back of the few example of 'Open the door' recorded early there lay a considerable body of song which had arisen among the folk" (1921: 576).

Psychologically, the "open the door" formula is an opportunity in the fictive expression of song to fantasize a sexual union that probably seems dangerous or defiant of authority. Toelken points out that the night-visit songs involve "invitation and negotiation, entry into a woman's chamber, cock-crow, and exit from chamber—more explicitly, verbal foreplay, sexual entry, ejaculation, and withdrawal" (1995: 64). The frequency with which the "cock" (*Hahn* in German) appears in the songs is an indication that the animal plays more than a practical role in the narrative, for it is, in Toelken's words, "one of the most common English metaphorical terms for penis, and both terms carry heavy implications for fertility and agricultural plenty" (1995: 63). The night-visit songs involving the barrier of the door distinguishing cultural space between inside and outside the "woman's chamber" were expressed in clearly symbolic language.

The night-visit as described in the "Barnacle Bill" narrative appears romantic, often intertwined with the idea of young lovers' tender union and parting before the brave man's death. As performed by sailors the suitor's visit implies sexual dalliance and bravado. Toelken presents the performance context of the sailor song "Rollin' Home," for example, as a different type from the night-visit, because its narrative outcome is an open reunion between the sailor out at sea for a long time with his sweetheart on shore. What he leaves behind on the way to the domestic scene of the civilized home is the erotic pleasure of exotic women associated with the open seas:

> Good-bye, you fair Hawaiian ladies,
> We must bid you all adieu,
> But we'll recall these pleasant hours,
> That we've often spent with you,

CHORUS
Rollin' home, rollin' home
Rollin' home across the sea,
Rollin' home to old New England
Rollin' home, dear land, to thee.

We will leave you our best wishes
As we leave your rocky shore;
We'll be sailin' home to Rockport,
And you won't see us anymore.
                    (Quoted from Toelken 1995: 54–55; see also Harlow 2004 [1962] 133–36;
                                        Hugill 1961:181–98; Palmer 1986: 116)

Although couched in metaphors, the lyrics sung by men for Toelken made the women present uncomfortable. According to the collector, the male singers understood "spent" in the first verse to mean penile ejaculation. Toelken adds that "everyone remembers that some sea captain in the family had explained that the phrase 'leaving your best wishes' meant having left a young woman pregnant" (1995: 54).

The symbolic association is clear that out on the open sea, the sailor is wild and virile, but on land his persona will change to being tame and domesticated. The song can raise heated words in performance as to how long the sailor can maintain that domestic state and how desirable it is (Toelken 1995: 54–55). Although the normative expectation is that the sailor should be overjoyed to be "home," narratives sung or told by sailors often express the sentiment of *Sailor Boy and Songs* (1852) that seamen "become so used to living on the water that when they are on land they sometimes do not know what to do with themselves to pass away their time. And after a few days or weeks they are very glad to be on board their ship again, and on the wide, blue sea" (1852: 3). So ill-equipped to be on land, they demonstrate in their fantasies both their naval as well as their masculine superiority with sexual dominance over women on shore.

Some analysts note a shift in the contemporary night-visit song epitomized by "Barnacle Bill" from the young couple of equivalent age to a predatory "dirty old man" pursuing a young woman. Annotating Vance Randolph's "unprintable" collection of folksongs, Legman makes a tie of the night-visitor theme, especially of the "pretty little miss" parody of the "pretty fair maid" to the mountaineer singing of "The Best Old Feller in the World" (no. 426) and "I'm Going Away to Texas" (no. 363). These two songs, involving a demure, loving woman, are answered curtly by an apparently uncaring older man who substitutes aggression for reprehensible sexuality.

Another relevant dialogue is in the frequently collected "Pretty Fair Maid in the Garden" (Laws N42; Sharp 98) involving a soldier or sailor who returns home in disguise to test the faithfulness of his sweetheart but finds his advances resisted by the maiden who will be true only to her lover (see Rennick 1963; Frank 1996; Green 1971). The loyal female who chides the visitor, "A man of honor you must be" may be the source for the "fair young maiden" characterization in the risque Barnacle Bill song.

Further suggesting "Barnacle Bill" as a ballad parody turned into a manly drinking anthem is the song's subversion of the many sentimental love ballads involving handsome Sweet (or Young) William (including "Pretty Fair Maid in the Garden," "Sweet William the Sailor Boy," and "Young William"). The anti-hero of an ignoble, unbecoming Bill is familiar from many songs featuring the boozing, womanizing, freewheeling "jolly tar" ("Sweet William the Sailor Boy" in Brewster 1940: 269–70, and Owens 1950: 134–35; "Rattling Jack" in Ashton 1891: 50; cf. *Vrolijke Zeeman*, or the Jolly Seaman, in Meertens Instituut). (During the Jazz Age of the 1920s, an allusion to the Sweet William of balladry was apparent in Jack Yellen's lyrics to "Big Bad Bill is Sweet William Now," first a vocal hit for Margaret Young in 1924 and again for Emmet Miller in 1929 and Peggy Lee in 1962. The song describes a rough, aggressive character, who after getting married, becomes a tranquil, domesticated person engaged in washing dishes and mopping the floor.)

A related parody of Sweet William and Fair Margaret (Child 74) found in music hall songsheets from the 1830s is "Paddy Whack," identified as a "favorite Irish Song." Lyrics of bawdy versions contain details of a "Rollicking Irishman" similar to the early verses of "Barnacle Bill" in which the anti-hero has the worried fair maiden on the floor:

> Young William threw Margery down on the floor,
> And with his stout gimblet began for to bore,
> But in the midst of his fibbing, and fumbling, and thumbing,
> "By my old smock," cries she, "there is somebody coming."
>
> But William kept driving, he was not afraid.
> Half dying with anguish, poor Margery said,
> "O lor, deary me, how you're stuffing and strumming,
> There's a foot on the stairs—there is somebody coming."   (Speaight 1975: 24)

William keeps driving, resulting in "that nature's soft stream flowed without any humming." At that point she announces, "'There—I told you,' says she, 'There was somebody coming.'" These lines compare to the fair young maiden's question to "Barnacle Bill" of "What's that running down your leg?" to which he replies, "It was a shot in the dark that missed its mark" or "It's the goo that comes with the screw" (Morgan 1969; Voorhis 1972).

Vance Randolph's bawdy parodic versions of "Pretty Little Miss" moved folklorist Frank Hoffman to assign a special erotic narrative motif to supplement Stith Thompson's T72, Woman won and then scorned: T72.0.2, Girl seduced by promise of marriage and then scorned after she becomes pregnant. This assignment loses sight, however, of the essential connection to the sailor's background, out on the "raging sea for years on end" coming ashore to be pleasured.

A structural if not motific connection can be made to the ancient story of the "sailor who went inland." In the *Odyssey* the sailor tiring of the seafarer's life is instructed to take a well-shaped oar and go inland until he reaches people who do not know the sea. When he encounters a traveler who does not know what the oar is, he settles down and makes a sacrifice to lord Poseidon. For this, he will enjoy a comfortable old age.

In modern erotic versions collected in the twentieth century that appear to undermine the message of the possibility of transitioning from the life of the sea to the land, the sailor goes to a farmhouse and asks to be put up for the night. When he asks a maiden in the house what he is holding in his hand, she innocently calls it a stick or "mother's pudding stick." The sailor beds (and sometimes marries) her and uses nautical metaphors to represent intercourse; in bed naked on her back, she explains "there's been a squall, and I've got everything clewed up. / Now I'm scudding on the bare poles."

In "Barnacle Bill," the fair maiden asks the sailor what he is carrying between his legs; he answers "It's only me pole to stick up your hole!" (Or "mast to stick up your ass"). The oar in this version becomes phallicized and is as crucial to the sailor's body and personality as it is a tool of his livelihood. Another connection may be in the allusion to "Rollicking" to represent being testicled, because the u-shaped "rowlocks" or oarlocks, the brace for the oar in which the rower exerts a thrust force, was British slang for male gonads (Page 1973: 40).

In a broadside from the 1840s printed by William Pratt of Birmingham, England, the sailor is Abraham Brown and the metaphorical use of the pole, mast, oar, or pin is similar.

> Who is it knocks at our door,
> Says a very nice young lady.
> Who is it &c.
> It's I myself and nobody else
> Says Abraham Brown the Sailor,
> It's I myself, &c.
>
> Oh! Open the door and let him in,
> Says this very nice young lady,
> And where am I to sleep to night
> Says Abraham Brown the Sailor
>
> You may sleep on my soft pincushion
> Says this very nice young lady
> And I've a pin, I'll run it in,
> Says Abraham Brown the Sailor
>
> I feel it rise between my [thighs]
> Says this very nice young lady,
> It's in your [quim] up to the rim,
> Says Abraham Brown the Sailor
>
> Ah! now it's in let it remain,
> Says this very nice young lady,
> I'll be d—d if I do, I shall want it again,
> Says Abraham Brown the Sailor
>
> When shall I have your pin again
> Says this very nice young lady
> When I can make it stand again,
> Says Abraham Brown the Sailor

The broadside does not credit anyone as composer for the verses and its tune is given as "My Heart and Lute" (probably the poetical ballad by Thomas Moore with music by Henry Bishop in 1830).

ABRAHAM
BROWN THE
SAILOR.

Tune—*My heart and Lute.*

Who is it knocks at our door,
Says a very nice young lady.
   Who is it &c.

It's I myself and nobody else,
Says Abraham Brown the Sailor,
   Ti's I myself, &c.

Oh ! open the door and let him in,
 Says this very nice young lady,
And where am I to sleep to night,
 Says Abraham Brown the Sailor

You may sleep on my soft pincush
  ion,
 Says this very nice young lady,
And I've a pin, I'll run it in,
 Says Abraham Brown the Sailor

I feel it rise between my——
 Says this very nice young lady,
It's in your—up to the rim,
 Says Abraham Brown the Sailor

Ah ! now it's in let it remain,
 Says this very nice young lady,
I'll be d—-d if I do, I shall want it
Says Abraham Brown &c.(again,

When shall I have your pin again ?
 Says this very nice young lady,
When I can make it stand again,
   Says Abraham Brown &c.

Broadside Of "Abraham Brown The Sailor" Printed By William Pratt, Birmingham, England, 1840s. (Courtesy Bodleian Library, University of Oxford)

Ballad tune for "My Heart And Lute" (composed by Henry Bishop, 1830)

In the twentieth century, maritime collector Joanna C. Colcord offered a forecastle song of "Abram (or Abel) Brown" in *Songs of American Sailormen* (1938) as the source of "Barnacle Bill the Sailor" broadcast over the radio with a different melody. She indicated that many more verses circulated but provided only what she considered "printable verses."

> Who's that knocking at my door?
> Who's that knocking at my door?
> Who's that knocking at my door?
> Cried the fair young maiden.
>
> Won't you come down and let me in?
> Cried Abram Brown the sailor.
>
> I'll come down and let you in,
> Cried the fair young maiden.
>
> Have you got a place for me to sleep?
> Cried Abram Brown the sailor. (1964: 178–79)

Colcord's version of Abraham Brown was a composite text jotted down from her memory. A field recorded text recorded on board a ship in 1929 from

Jack Taylor of Newfoundland was transcribed by Elizabeth Bristol Greenleaf and Grace Yarrow Mansfield.

> "Who is that knocking at my door?"
> Cried the fair young lady. (*Repeat these two lines*)
>
> It's I meself and nobody else,"
> Said Abram Brown the sailor. (*Repeat these two lines*)
>
> "May I come down and let you in?"
> Cried the fair young lady (*Repeat these two lines*)
>
> "I'm afraid the bed isn't big enough."
> Cried Abram Brown the sailor. (*Repeat these two lines*)
>
> (Greenleaf and Mansfield 1933: 105)

The singer likely cleaned up his rendition for the women collectors or did not complete it, because the narrative appears to stop short. Former sailor Stan Hugill commented in his collection that the song was "entirely obscene." He learned it on his first voyage to sea before World War II (440). Taylor told Greenleaf and Mansfield that he picked up the song twenty years before he sang it for them, placing it in the early twentieth century.

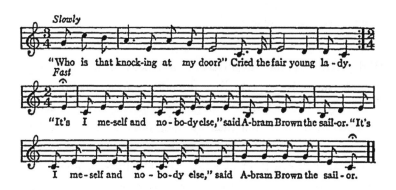

Tune for "Abram Brown the Sailor" as sung by Jack Taylor of Newfoundland (Greenleaf and Mansfield 1933: 105)

In an apparent indication of the song's diffusion, Greenleaf and Mansfield mentioned that John Lomax had collected "Abram Brown" in the American west, although he did not publish the song. Frederick Pease Harlow's comment was that it was primarily a "popular pumping chantey typical of the drunken sailor ashore going out to 'paint the town red.'" (166). Hugill recalled the performance of "Abram Brown" on board ship this way: "This shanty would often be sung by two soloists or shantymen in similar manner to *Mobile Bay* and *Billy Boy*, one singer for the questions and one for the answers" (333). In "Billy Boy," the young sailor finds a maiden who he wants to marry but she "cannot leave her mother." Billy is being mocked in the performance for being tied down on land by women rather than being free on the ocean. Marriage also frequently results in "Mobile Bay" after seeking out many women in different ports. Another dialogue song from sailors is "Saucy (or Tarry) Sailor" that also features a seafarer "who has just returned from sea." The maiden refuses him because she says that sailors are dirty, ragged, and "saucy." He tells her that he has money and she changes her attitude. The sailor scolds her and boasts again that he could have other women,

> "Do you take me to be foolish?
> Do you think I am mad?
> That I'd wed the like of you, miss,
> When there's others to be had?
>
> "No! I'll cross the briny ocean,
> No! My boat shall spread her wing;
> You refused me, ragged, dirty,
> Not for you the wedding ring."

(Gould and Sharp 1907: 76–77).

With a narrative, the categorization of "Abel Brown" and "Saucy Sailor" as drinking songs is suspect. They do not mention alcohol and do not lend themselves to toasting. The singing of the songs may indeed may be accompanied by drinking but their meaning does not appear to be defined by it.

To put "Abel Brown the Sailor" in print, Hugill bowdlerized the words. With twelve verses, his version is more extensive than Colcord's. He speculates that the name "Abel Brown" comes from the common initialism among sailors of "Able-Bodied Seamen" (see also Morgan 2002: 18).

> Oh, where am I going' to sleep to-night?
> Sez Abel Brown the Sailor! (Repeat)
>
> You can sleep up on the mast,
> Cried the fair young maiden! (Repeat)
>
> Oh, the mat is rough an' me skin ain't tough,
> Sez Abel Brown the Sailor! (Repeat)

You can sleep upon the shelf,
Cried the fair young maiden! (Repeat)

What 'ave yer got upon the shelf?
Sez Abel Brown the Sailor (Repeat)

I've got some rum upon the shelf,
Cried the fair young maiden. (Repeat)

Me throat is long an' me thirst is strong,
Sez Abel Brown the Sailor (Repeat)

What if you roll from off the shelf?
Cried the fair young maiden (Repeat)

I'll bounce on the floor an' ask for more,
Sez Abel Brown the Sailor (Repeat)

What if the police should come to the house?
Cried the fair young maiden (Repeat)

I'll take 'em on in twos and three's,
Sez Abel Brown the Sailor (Repeat)

Then I'll let you stay with me,
Cried the fair young maiden (Repeat).

Although the names Abraham Brown and Abel Brown appear a long way off from Bollicky and Barnacle Bill, a connection exists in their shared reference to vernacular, rough-around-the-edges qualities of the characters. Both are wanderers who will not settle down and both appear in literature through the nineteenth century in reference to sailor types, usually representing more experienced sailors in contrast to young "Jack Tars." John Camden Hotten defines "Abraham Man" in *The Slang Dictionary* (1874) as current argot for a wanderer or vagabond and cites a precedent in Shakespeare's *King Lear* of "Abram-man" for beggar. Abraham Brown shows up in British literature as a stock name for a common sailor.

In William Knox Wigram's *Five Hundred Pounds Reward* (1868), the captain chastises the common sailor named Abraham Brown for not following regulations but then he turns out to be a hero saving the ship. The captain responds afterward by saying, "When our officers desire to confer the highest mark of approval upon a sailor whose agility, integrity, and general worth appear to entitle him to distinction, they know no higher encomium than that conveyed in these simple words: 'Let him be rated as an A.B. [Able-Bodied Seaman]'" (Wigram 1868: 58).

The suggestion of the sailor as a shady, marginal character comes through in the assignment of the earthy, racialized, or even scatological "Brown" as his last name, as it does in the popular sailor song "Sally Brown" about a wild mulatto woman who "drinks rum and chews tobacco" and significantly, "wouldn't marry." (A related appellation is in the Child ballad 98, "Brown Adam the Smith," in which the loner returns from his hunting and cuts off the hand of a knight trying to persuade Adam's lady to leave.)

"Abram Brown" in song was often designated "the sailor" probably to distinguish it from the nursery rhyme "Old Abram Brown" who is "dead and gone, You'll never see him more; He used to wear a long brown coat, That buttoned down before" (Opie and Opie 1997: 58–59). Although the namesakes appear to be different, they share a characterization as old and differentially dressed, perhaps indicating their shared social marginalization.

No doubt the moniker of "Bollicky Bill" was off-color and apparently in vogue by British soldiers and sailors for the song by the end of the nineteenth century. One might speculate about the relation of this alliterative name to the fame for Buffalo Bill who toured Europe as well as America from 1872 to 1890. Indeed, one of the variants collected in the University of California Berkeley Folklore Archives is "Buffalo Bill the Sailor" with the words, "It's Buffalo Bill from over the hill, said Buffalo Bill the Sailor" (Visweswaran 1981).

There might be more connection between Barnacle and Buffalo Bill than the rhythmic sound produced by uttering their name. Both characters benefited from the publicity given them by popular dime-novel writer Ned Buntline. Buntline was a pseudonym for Edward Judson who had run away to sea to work as a cabin boy aboard a Navy ship in 1834 (Monaghan 1951: 34–43). He mined his sea experiences for pirate novels before traveling inland into the American frontier in 1869 to build up William Cody as Buffalo Bill, "the king of the border men" in the *New York Weekly* (Buntline 1881). Buntline built Cody into a hyper-masculine rugged adventurer who set out in the "wild west" as the nation's greatest scout. He used the same newspaper as an outlet for adventures of "Barnacle Bill" (1873). It was headlined on the front page "A Wild, Strange and Romantic Story of the Sea." (Buntline 1873a) Undoubtedly, Buntline hoped for Barnacle Bill to achieve the popular status of William Cody, but he did not have a real-life Bill to trot out on stage.

Still, the likelihood exists that the Barnacle moniker circulated as a result of Buntline's story concerning an old man named Barnacle Bill who recalls sea battles to save the daughter of his "deadliest foe," the Earl of Cardigan. Rather than being seductive, however, this Bill appears nobly heroic when he storms in past the cabin door. Buntline wrote that Bill explains to a young sailor, "I sprang into the cabin. I wrenched the chains from the limbs of the prostrate earl. I pointed him to the open arm chest, just as a wild, heart-chilling shriek came ringing from that inner cabin; then as *I* would have leaped forward to aid her in that dark moment, she—the earl's daughter—sprang out of the cabin with a blood-stained dagger in her hand, shrieking: 'Back—*back* or die as he died!' (Buntline 1873b: 2).

A possible source for Buntline was a report of an "old hermit called 'Barnacle Bill'" in St. Johns, Newfoundland. As reported in New York and other newspapers, Barnacle Bill had been a sailor and become a recluse. The *New York Sun* characterized him as "the old savage," and described his "chamber of horrors" containing nine women's corpses in his cabin, including that of a "young lady who belonged to a wealthy family in the Bay of Islands" ("A Wrecker" 1871: 1; "Horrible Deeds": 9). A year later, a hurricane destroyed fishery vessels along the Newfoundland coast though a correspondent wrote the *New York Evening Post* that the coverage of the event was "a gross fabrication." It had evidently by the same hand that manufactured the tale of "Barnacle Bill," (See both "The Wreck at the Shoots," and "The Great Storm on Labrador" ("The Seal-Fishery Disasters" 1872: 1). Apparently, the writer assumed that readers knew the story and the name of Barnacle Bill as popularized by Buntline.

Most civilians considered Barnacle or Buffalo more polite than Bollicky or Rollicky, both referring to testes (Randolph 1992: 791). A "barnacle back" in sailor slang referred to old sailors and a barnacle to a group carried the implication of being unwanted (Shay 1991: 381). A singer of "Barnacle Bill" interviewed by a folklore collector at the University of California at Berkeley commented that "the sailor was 'old and fat' because barnacles are also 'old and crusty' (Sauls 1981).

This interpretation suggests a number of other oppositions besides feminine and masculine: old philandering, rotund man to the young loyal, slender maiden. Barnacles may also have a sublimated meaning in relation to sailors having an image of being both feminine and masculine because barnacles have a hermaphroditic body and are known by sailors to have extraordinarily long penises, the largest in relation to body size in the animal kingdom. Yet a female singer of the song at Berkeley who learned the lyrics from her mother thought "barnacles looked like little vaginas" (Sauls 1981).

Some real-life characters vie for the distinction of being models for the song's male protagonist. William Henry Taylor (1855–1900) was a pitcher in major league baseball from 1881 until 1887 who went by the nickname of "Bollicky Bill." He did not sport a huge frame (180 cm, 93 kgs) and mention is not made in chronicles of his testicular size or sailing background, but he was frequently fined for drunkenness and rowdyism (Nemec 2004: 48). Another claim is for William Bernard, a rough nineteenth-century sailor who came to San Francisco to cash in on the California Gold Rush in 1849 and apparently made a name for himself by raising a ruckus. According to legendary accounts, he went by the name of Barnacle Bill (Boyes 1936). A possibility, however, is that the moniker became attached to these larger-than-life characters because the song was already in circulation. The circulation of the name Barnacle Bill in early twentieth century popular culture is apparent from silent films such as *The Sea Urchin* (1913) with Lon Chaney playing the role of Barnacle Bill and *The Comeback of Barnacle Bill* (1918; an African-American film set in Chicago). *Punch*, the famous British humor magazine, published "The Barnacle (A Sort of Sea Shanty)" by "A.P.H." in 1920. Its opening lines about the seaworthiness of a sailor type are "Old Bill Barnacle sticks to his ship, He never is ill on the stormiest trip, Upside down he crosses the ocean, If you do that you enjoy the motion" (455).

The first printed lyrics under the heading of "Bollochy Bill" appeared in 1927 in *Immortalia* compiled by "A Gentleman Around Town." It fits the outline of my third song type of the resistant maiden who incrementally gives in to the sailor's advances.

> "Who is knocking at my door,"
> Said the fair young maiden.
> "Who is knocking at my door,"
> Said the fair young maiden.
>
> "Open the door and let me in,"
> Said Ballochy Bill the sailor;
> "Open the door and let me in,"
> Said Ballochy Bill the sailor.

"You may sleep upon the floor,"
Said the fair young maiden.
"To hell with the floor, I can't fuck that,"
Said Ballochy Bill the sailor.

"You may lie down at my side,"
Said the fair young maiden.
"To hell with your side, I can't fuck that,"
Said Ballochy Bill the sailor.

"You may lie between my thighs,"
Said the fair young maiden.
"What've you got between your thighs?"
Said Ballochy Bill the sailor.

"O, I've got a nice pin-cushion,"
Said the fair young maiden.
"And I've got a pin that will just fit in,"
Said Ballochy Bill the sailor.

"But what if we have a baby?"
Said the fair young maiden.
"Strangle the bastard and throw him away,"
Said Ballochy Bill the sailor.

"But what about the law, sir,"
Said the fair young maiden.
"Kick the bleeders out on their ass,"
Said Ballochy Bill the sailor.

"But what if there's an inquest?"
Said the fair young maiden.
"Then shove the inquest up your cunt,"
Said Ballochy Bill the sailor.

"And what about my paw and maw?"
Said the fair young maiden.
"Fuck your maw, and bugger your paw,"
Said Ballochy Bill the sailor.

"Whenever shall I see you?"
Said the fair young maiden.
"Whenever shall I see you?"
Said the fair young maiden.

"Never no more you dirty whore,"
Said Ballochy Bill the sailor.
"Never no more you dirty whore,"
Said Ballochy Bill the sailor.

The circumstances of the private printing of one thousand copies by the "Gentleman about Town" are still a mystery, but the subtitle gives the impression that the material was compiled from oral tradition, for it refers to risque ballads and songs "now for the first time brought together in book form" (see Baker and Bronner 2005: 317–18). Harold Bennett later confirmed that "Bollocky Bill the Sailor" with similar metaphors and scenarios (pin cushion, mat, inquest, pregnancy) circulated orally among British servicemen in World War II (2000: 68).

A year after *Immortalia* came out, Frank Shay included "Rollicking Bill the Sailor" for a trade publisher in *More Pious Friends and Drunken Companions*. He only included three verses, suggesting the second "Bill" type involving the protest "we have only one bed!" He teases the reader, however, by stating that "there are many versions, all of them far better than the appended sample" (151). He makes no mention of the tune, but in 1929 another privately printed collection titled *A Collection of Sea Songs and Ditties from the Stores of Dave E. Jones* included words to "Bollicky Bill" (fitting my outline of type 3) "sung to the tune of 'Barnacle Bill the Sailor.'"

> Who's that knocking at my door, said the fair young maiden
> Who's that knocking at my door, said the fair young miaden
> 'Tis only I, 'tis only I, said Bollicky Bill the sailor,
> I'll come down and let you in, said the fair young maiden
> I'll come down and let you in, said the fair young maiden,
> And what do I get if I do come in, said Bollicky Bill the sailor,
> I've a cushion between my thighs, said the fair young maiden
> I've a cushion between my thighs, said the fair young maiden
> And I've got a pin that will just fit in, said Bollicky Bill the sailor,
> What if I should have a child, said the fair young maiden,
> What if we should have a child, said the fair young maiden,
> Wring the neck of the son of a bitch, said Bollicky Bill the sailor.

The reference to the tune probably is to the recording hit by Frank Luther and Carson Robison for "Barnacle Bill the Sailor" first released in January 1929. (The pair known for working with country songs and old-time ballads recorded no fewer than thirteen other versions or sequels to "Barnacle Bill "under a number of pseudonyms between 1929 and 1934.) The song was covered by other American popular artists including Vernon Dalhart (1929), Hoagy Carmichael (1930), Louis Jordan (1938), and Nat Gonella (1942).

Sheet music to "Barnacle Bill the Sailor" by Carson Robison and Frank Luther (Peer International, 1929).

The song shows up quickly after the American hit was released in Australian commercial recordings by Len Maurice (1929) and Tex Morton (1937). In the United Kingdom, popular actor and music-hall singer Bobbie Comber issued "Barnacle Bill the Sailor" in 1929, followed by "The Return of Barnacle Bill the Sailor" that same year. The song was also associated with the national radio shows of Singin' Sam, the Barbasol Man (Harry Frankel) on WABC in New York, beginning in 1931. In a 1949 review of Frank Shay's *American Songs and Chanteys from the Days of Iron Men and Wood Ships*, folklorist Horace Beck noted that Shay's "Rollicking Bill the Sailor" reminded him of "Singing Sam, the radio singer" who had performed the song as "Barnacle Bill the Sailor" (1949: 332). Sailors sing a bowdlerized version of "Barnacle Bill" in the movie *Dames Ahoy* (1930) around the plot of three seamen searching for a blonde who swindled them.

The song was also featured in cartoons for Popeye the Sailor Man (1935; the rotund, bearded Bluto is in the role of Barnacle Bill) and Betty Boop (1930; dark-faced Bimbo is Barnacle Bill). In the UK, prolific English filmmaker Harry Hughes directed the popular movie *Barnacle Bill* (1935). In 1941, American director Richard Thorpe adapted the film for Hollywood studio MGM with Wallace Beery playing the salty lead who evades matrimony while obeying his matriarchal Aunt Letty on the ship. The name again was

In the above movie still from "Barnacle Bill" (Metro-Goldwyn-Mayer, 1941), the Bill character played by Wallace Beery is served by a stern matriarch Aunt Letty (played by Sara Haden) who dominates him.

prominently featured in the title of a British film starring Alec Guiness as Captain William "Barnacle Bill" Horatio Ambrose, although the release in America was billed as *All at Sea*. The popular association of "Barnacle Bill" with the manly aggressiveness of seafarers was evident in the national press's attention to star Navy football player William S. "Barnacle Bill" Busik during the early 1940s. According to his obituary in 2005, the name was a "spinoff from the ditty, 'He's rough and tough and knows his stuff, he's Barnacle Bill the sailor" (Kelly 2005).

Luther and Robison copyrighted their song "Barnacle Bill the Sailor" and Peer International published the sheet music in 1929. Their "composition" is an adjustment of the sailor's replies to five lines from the traditional repeated two lines. After the familiar "who's that knocking at my door" opening, it follows generally the outline of type I of the traditional song, but it also contains unprecedented verses of sailor cliches and references to being lit up like a Christmas tree.

> Who's that knocking at my door?
> Who's that knocking at my door?
> Who's that knocking at my door, cried the fair young maiden.
>
> It's only me from over the sea, said Barnacle Bill the sailor
> I'm all dressed up like a Christmas tree, said Barnacle Bill the sailor
> I'll sail the sea until I croak
> I'll fight and swear and chew and smoke
> But I can't swim a bloomin' stroke! said Barnacle Bill the sailor
>
> Are you young and handsome sir?
> Are you young and handsome sir?
> Are you young and handsome sir, cried the fair young maiden?
>
> I'm old and rough and mean and tough! said Barnacle Bill the sailor.
> I never can git rough enough, said Barnacle Bill the sailor
> Why I can whip a dozen men
> And my age must be a hundred and ten
> And now I'm startin' all over again! Said Barnacle Bill the sailor.
>
> I'll come down and let you in
> I'll come down and let you in
> I'll come down and let you in, cried the fair young maiden
>
> Well hurry before I bust in the door, said Barnacle Bill the sailor
> I'll rare and tear and rant and roar, said Barnacle Bill the sailor
> I'll spin yuh yarns and tell yuh lies

I'll drink your coffee and eat your pies
I'll kiss your cheeks and black your eyes, said Barnacle Bill the sailor

Sing me a love song low and sweet
Sing me a love song low and sweet
Oh! Sing me a love song low and sweet, cried the fair young maiden
Oh! Sixteen men on a dead man's chest, sang Barnacle Bill the sailor
Yo he ho and a bottle of rum, sang Barnacle Bill the sailor
Oh high rig a jig and a jaunting car
A he a ho are you most done
Hurray my boys let the bull-jane run! sang Barnacle Bill the sailor

Tell me that we soon shall wed
Tell me that we soon shall wed
Tell me that we soon shall wed, cried the fair young maiden

I've got a gal in every port! said Barnacle Bill the sailor
The handsome gals is what I court! said Barnacle Bill the sailor
With my false heart and flatterin' tongue
I courts 'em all both old and young
I courts 'em all and marries none! said Barnacle Bill the sailor

When shall I see you again?
When shall I see you again?
When shall I see you again? Cried the fair young maiden

Never again I'll come no more! said Barnacle Bill the sailor
Tonight I'm sailin' from the shore, said Barnacle Bill the sailor
If you wait for me to come
Settin' and waitin' and suckin' yer thumb
You'll wait until the day of your doom! said Barnacle Bill the sailor

(Spoken) "Goodbye"

The song is devoid of overt sexual references but contains plenty of aggression by Bill in contrast to the sweetness of the fair young maiden who desires marriage. Bill belongs to the sea, however, where he can "fight and swear and chew and smoke." With his wandering, he brags that he has a woman in every port, apparently much to the disappointment of the maiden.

Robison and Luther's copyrighted text can be compared with a number of oral versions collected before 1927. While editing the "Old Songs that Men Have Sung" column for *Adventure Magazine*, Robert Winslow Gordon (1888–1961), founding head of the Archive of American Folk Song at the Library of Congress, received a version of "Bollocky Bill the Sailor" on September 17, 1923 from E.S. Fowlds of Hidalgo, Mexico, some years before the Luther-Robison recording.

> Who's that knocking at the door?
> Said the fair young maiden
> Who's that knocking at the door?
> Said the fair young maiden.
> O it's you lover come home from sea
> Said Bollocky Bill the sailor.
> O it's your lover come home from sea
> Said Bollocky Bill the sailor.
>
> When will you be back once more
> O never again, you poxy old whore.

Gordon did not select the song for his column and buried the text in a private file he labeled "inferno" for bawdy texts. Others during the 1920s followed, including the following text labeled "Bolakee Bill the Sailor" from a "Cousin Jack."

> Oh who's that knocking at my door
> Says the fair young maiden.
> Oh who's that knocking at my door
> Says the fair young maiden.
>
> Oh this is me and no one else
> Says Bolakee Bill the sailor.
>
> I'll open the door and let you in
> Says the fair young maiden.
>
> Now I am here I'll stay till dawn
> Says Bolakee Bill the sailor.
>
> But a babe now I shall have
> Says the fair young maiden.
>
> But it will never see its daddy
> Says Bolakee Bill the sailor.
>
> And if it be a lass
> Says the fair young maiden.
>
> Strangle it as soon as its born
> Says Bolakee Bill the sailor.
>
> But if it be a laddie
> Says the fair young maiden.

Send him out to sea
Says Bolakee Bill the sailor.

I'll make him bell bottom trousers
Says the fair young maiden.

Get him a suit of navy blue
Says Bolakee Bill the sailor.

And he will climb the riggings
Says the fair young maiden.

Like his daddy used to do
Says Bolakee Bill the sailor.

The song shows a connection to "Bell Bottom Trousers" with the "suit of navy blue, Let him climb the rigging like his daddy used to do" (Cray 1992: 73). Using the same title, the same performer contributed a second version that has a formulaic opening characteristic of other ballads more commonly known as "The Lass that Loved a Sailor" or "Never Trust a Sailor" (Johnson, John 1935: 51; Randolph 1980: IV, 328–29). Unlike Cousin Jack's first version, his second takes the perspective of a woman:

How all you woman folks
Listen now to me
Do not trust a sailor
An inch above your knee

Take my advice
And keep them from your homes
For they always cause trouble
And soon they will roam.

Cousin Jack stopped at that point and commented, "Some of the words are pretty raw so I have altered them, also a line or two." The text is comparable to a contribution Gordon received from John L. Bracken stationed at sea on October 20, 1923.

Never let a sailor boy get an inch above your knee.
I'd dress him up in a sailor suit and sent him off to sea.

Adding to the variety of songs with the chorus of "Who's that knocking at my door?" in Gordon's file is a letter from William F. Burroughs dated March 20, 1925 with the heading of "The Fair Young Maiden" fitting the outline of my third type. Instead of Bollicky Bill as the sailor, it introduces the name of Abram Brown.

"Who's that knocking at my door?"
Said the fair young maiden.
"Who's that knocking at my door?"
Said the fair young maiden.

"It's me an' I wanna get in,"
Said Abram Brown the sailor.
"It's me an' I wanna get in,"
Said Abram Brown the sailor.

"Open the door and walk in,"
Said the fair young maiden.
"Open the door and walk in,"
Said the fair young maiden.

"There's only room in the bed for one,"
Said Abram Brown the sailor,
"There's only room in the bed for one,"
Said Abram Brown the sailor.

"You can sleep between my thighs,"
Said the fair young maiden.
"You can sleep between my thighs,"
Said the fair young maiden.

"What is that hairy thing I see?"
Said Abram Brown the sailor.
"What is that hairy thing I see?"
Said Abram Brown the sailor.

"That is my pin cushion,"
Said the fair young maiden.
"That is my pin cushion,"
Said the fair young maiden.

"I have the pin and it must go in,"
Said Abram Brown the sailor.
"I have the pin and it must go in,"
Said Abram Brown the sailor.

"What if we should have a child?"
Said the fair young maiden.
"What if we should have a child,"
Said the fair young maiden.

"I'd kill the dirty son of a bitch,"
Said Abram Brown the sailor.
"I'd kill the dirty son of a bitch,"
Said Abram Brown the sailor.

Distinguishing the text is its use of dialogue set in an alternate verse structure. Although not many ballads are set this way, the format is comparable to the more widely reported "Our Good Man" or "Three Nights Drunk" (Child 274) using the dialogue structure. Indeed, L.C. Lockley of Berkeley, California, in May, 1923, contributed along with a version of Barnacle Bill a version of Child 274 he called "A Sailor Man Came Home One Night as Drunk as Drunk Could Be." (In other collections it is called "The Sailor's Return.") Even if not many of the Child ballads use this structure, the form carries popular appeal. Indeed, in Joseph Hickerson's estimation, the "Goodman" song stands as among the most popular of the English and Scottish classic ballads in oral tradition (Cray 1992: 19–20). Other ballad traditions using dialogue related to a theme of tense courtship between apparently oppositional characters are the widely reported "The Quaker's Courtship" and "The Frog and the Mouse" (Froggie Went a-Courtin') (see Randolph 1980: I, 55–63 [song no. 108]; III, 402–10 [song no. 362]; Roud [716 for Quaker's Courtship and 16 for Frog Went a-Courtin'].)

Of significance are songs associated with Barnacle Bill or Abram Brown. "Bang Bang Lulu" was frequently reported as bawdy material sung by men, and especially sailing men, in later collections, including *Immortalia*. The same informant who provided Abram Brown, for example, followed immediately with "Lulu," containing the chorus:

Oh bang way on Lulu
Oh bang her good and strong,
For what are you gonna do for your banging
When Lulu's dead and gone?

Perhaps the reason for its association with Barnacle Bill is not only its aggressive sexuality but also a lyrical reference to the consequence of a baby from intercourse:

Oh Lulu had a baby
She called him Sunny Dick
She couldn't call it Lulu
'Cause it didn't have no [dick].

Gordon also received a variant from Bill Nice of New Jersey on May 31, 1925, who recalled it from military duty in France during WWI:

My Lulu had a baby
His name was Sunny Jim
She put him in a bath tub (?)
To see if he could swim.

I wish I was a diamond ring
Upon my Lula's hand
'Cause every time she ------- [sic]
I'd see the promised land.

O bang away my Lulu
Bang away good and strong.
What you going to do for your banging away
When your Lulu's dead and gone?

The lyrics relate to a children's rhyme about an unwed mother still in British-American oral tradition as "Lulu [or Susie] had a baby, She named him Tiny Tim, She put him in the bathtub to see if he could swim" (Bronner 1988: 60–61; Cray 174). The song depends on the image of immersion in bathtub water aligned with a mother's care in contrast to as a sign of immaturity or feminization. The rebellious child in the children's verse "drank up all the water, He ate up all the soap, He tried to eat the bathtub, But it wouldn't go down his throat" (Bronner 1988: 60)

A ballad commonplace of the "lily white bed" is evident in a version identified as "Bollicky Bill the Sailor" contributed by J. F. McGinnis of Brooklyn, New York, to Gordon on November 20, 1926. The singer left out the door-knocking opening, but retained the narrative core of the request to sleep with the maiden.

Oh! where will I sleep to-night, fair maid,
Said Bollicky Bill, the Sailor,
You'll sleep in my bed, the maiden said,
To Bollicky Bill, the Sailor.

He went up stairs to her lily white bed,
Did Bollicky Bill, the Sailor,
He took the pillow from under her head,
And put it under her ass, instead,
Did Bollicky Bill, the Sailor.

Only one instance in the collection occurs of "Bocardy Bill," probably a reference to Bacardi rum of the West Indies, thus implying the character's drunkenness and association with the pirate-infested Caribbean. The contributor is not identified but use of the slang term "bugger" in the lyrics below suggests a Canadian or British source. An identical use of the "bugger the police" line is reported from oral tradition among Canadian and British servicemen (Bennett 2000: 68; Hopkins 1979: 151). In those sources, the line is followed by "But if there should be an inquest? / Stuff the inquest up your arse. / When shall I see you again? / Never no more, you fucking whore" (Hopkins 1979: 151; Bennett 2000: 68; Lyra Ebriosa 1933: 19).

> What have you got between your legs?
> Said Bocardy Bill the Sailor.
> What have you got between your legs?
> Said Bocardy Bill the Sailor.
>
> I have got a cushion there,
> Said the fair young maiden,
> I have got a cushion there,
> Said the fair young maiden.
>
> What if there should be a child,
> Said the fair young maiden.
>
> Strangle the bugger as soon as he comes
> Said Bocardy Bill the Sailor.
>
> What about the police force,
> Said the fair young maiden.
>
> Bugger the police and fuck the force,
> Said Bocardy Bill the Sailor.

In the above text, the "knocking" opening has been omitted, but the narrative sequence is still apparent in the pregnancy theme characteristic of the song's third type.

A performance context that I encounter in my contemporary collections is indicated by a 1924 rendition of "Abram Brown the Sailor" from R. M. Davids from Florida in which he notes that the male parts are rendered in a deep voice and sung quickly. The woman's part is often sung in a falsetto voice (see Colcord 1964: 179; Cray 1992: 81–82; Patrick 2006).

Who is that knocking at my door?
Cries the fair young maiden.
Who is that knocking at my door?
Cries the fair young maiden

Won't you come down and let me in?
Cried Abram Brown the sailor —*Bass voice; repeat.*

Oh, I'll come down and let you in,
Cries the fair young maiden.

Have you got a place for me to sleep?
Cries Abram Brown the sailor.

You can sleep by the side of me,
Cries the fair young maiden.

Oh, what have you got between your legs?
Cried Abram Brown the sailor.

I've got a hairy pin-cushion,
Cried the fair young maiden.

I've got a pin and I'll stick it in,
Cried Abram Brown the sailor.

If you stick it in you'll break my heart,
Cried the fair young maiden.

I'll break your heart or I'll make you fart,
Cried Abram Brown the sailor.

When can I have this treat again?
Cried the fair young maiden.

When you can get my cock to start
Cried Abram Brown the sailor.

How can I get your cock to stand?
Cried the fair young maiden.

Scratch my arse and tickle my balls,
Cried Abram Brown the sailor.

The oral versions in folklore archives at the end of the twentieth century rarely refer to Robison and Luther's verses about the Christmas tree or their form of the five-line reply. At the time the texts were collected, Barnacle Bill had become standardized as a title. Most versions are six to ten verses long, with the longest, deposited in archives at Indiana State University, at Berkeley, and at Oregon, totaling 22 verses. Contextual notes, however, suggest that in performance in summer camps, at rugby celebrations, and parties, the song can be substantially extended with communal improvisation (see Linton 1965: 115–17).

The second narrative type, of obstacles to Bill's advances, is the most common, followed by the third type, of metaphors for sexual acts used by the maiden. The first type, of the promise of marriage, rarely appears in university folklore archives. Although men contribute most of the items, a number are provided by women. Of the fourth type, which I suspect is a new feminist adaptation, the following is an example deposited in the Indiana State University Folklore Archives in 1974.

> Who's that knocking at my door?
> Who's that knocking at my door?
> Who's that knocking at my door?
> Said the fair young maiden.
>
> Open the door and fuck some more
> Said Barnacle Bill the sailor
> Open the door and fuck some more
> Said Barnacle Bill the sailor
>
> Are we going to the dance?
> Are we going to the dance?
> Are we going to the dance?
> Asked the fair young maiden.
>
> The hell with the dance, and off with the pants
> Said Barnacle Bill the sailor
> The hell with the dance, and off with the pants,
> Said Barnacle Bill the sailor.
>
> What if ma and pa find out?
> What if ma and pa find out?
> What if ma and pa find out?
> Asked the fair young maiden.
>
> We'll kill your pa and rape your ma
> Said Barnacle Bill the sailor
> We'll kill your pa and rape your ma
> Said Barnacle Bill the sailor.

What if we should have a child?
What if we should have a child?
What if we should have a child?
Asked the fair young maiden.

We'll dig a ditch and bury the bitch
Said Barnacle Bill the sailor
We'll dig a ditch and bury the bitch
Said Barnacle Bill the sailor.

What if you should get the chair?
What if you should get the chair?
What if you should get the chair?
Asked the fair young maiden.

I'll let a fart and blow it apart
Said Barnacle Bill the sailor
I'll let a fart and blow it apart
Said Barnacle Bill the sailor.

My vagina's much too tight
My vagina's much too tight
My vagina's much too tight
Said the fair young maiden.

I'll shove in my rod and give it a prod
Said Barnacle Bill the sailor
I'll shove in my rod and give it a prod
Said Barnacle bill the sailor.

What's that between your legs?
What's that between your legs?
What's that between your legs?
Asked the fair young maiden.

Give me a blow and watch it grow
Said Barnacle Bill the sailor
Give me a blow and watch it grow
Said Barnacle Bill the sailor.

Why are we lying on the bed?
Why are we lying on the bed?
Why are we lying on the bed?
Asked the fair young maiden.

Get on your back and open your crack
Said Barnacle Bill the sailor
Get on your back and open your crack
Said Barnacle Bill the sailor.

That was really very nice
That was really very nice
That was really very nice
Said the fair young maiden.

Roll over and then I'll do it again
Said Barnacle Bill the sailor
Roll over and then I'll do it again
Said Barnacle Bill the sailor.

Only twice is not enough
Only twice is not enough
Only twice is not enough
Said the fair young maiden

I'm too fucking tired to really get fired
Said Barnacle Bill the sailor
I'm too fucking tired to really get fired
Said Barnacle Bill the sailor

Get back up on top or I'll call the cops
Get back up on top or I'll call the cops
Get back up on top or I'll call the cops
Said the fair young maiden.

I'll do what I can, but I'm only a man
Said Barnacle Bill the sailor
I'll do what I can, but I'm only a man
Said Barnacle Bill the sailor.

Aren't you ever satisfied?
Aren't you ever satisfied?
Aren't you ever satisfied?
Said the tired young sailor.

Make it swell and fuck me to hell
Said Barnacle Bess the nimpho
Make it swell and fuck me to hell
Said Barnacle Bess the nimpho.

(Anonymous 1974)

A notable difference in this version is that the perspective is a female's, clearly in response the perception that the song is associated with men. Although the song features a dialogue of two characters, the male voice establishes Barnacle Bill as the admired hero because he is intrusive. He breaks down barriers and defies societal norms. Yet in setting up a structure in obverse form, the singer shows awareness of different gender expectations.

The first-person vantage of "Bell Bottom Trousers" (female) and "Maid of Amsterdam" (male) presents cautionary tales in contrast to Barnacle Bill's fantasy that invites participatory comment. Identified frequently as a drinking song, the play frame signaled by liquored release of decorum allows for exaggeration of the fantasy. Perhaps in that context, the song provides a warning in many collegiate contexts of violent or risky sexual behavior under the influence of alcohol, but the narrative content of the song suggests a consideration of other relationships.

The argument in song sets up a question for audience members as to which character will triumph. More than a courtship argument between man and woman, the song raises several oppositions that are left unmediated between the bollocky, barnacled, unattractive male and the demure, sweet, pretty maiden: old and young, wild and tame, rebellious and submissive, settled and wandering, home and away, and land and water.

CONTEXTS AND SYMBOLS

American college students who contributed Barnacle Bill songs to folklore archives frequently refer to first learning the song in summer camp and finding it revived in collegiate social events of fraternity parties, celebrations of male sports teams, and bar scenes (see Reuss 1965: 240–43). Documentation of versions from the United Kingdom and Australia repeatedly mentions young men singing the song at rugby team gatherings (see Rugby Songs 2007: 3). The kinds of play frames in these contexts often allow expressions of manliness that would appear exaggerated in other settings. They are typically all-male groups who are usually aware of cultural pressures on them to be tough and strong as expected male roles, and yet at the same time deferential to women.

The timing of the song's performance in the life course suggests the use of the fantasized text at a time of pubertal development and sexual awareness, often as compensation for insecurity about expressing sexual desire. For pre-adolescent boys particularly, a factor in folkloric practices is the son's relationship to his mother, for males in order to mature want to show that they are no longer "mama's boys." It is more important for them to separate from the mother than from the father, and a folkloric way to do that is to declare sexual, violent dominance over women or the mothers of peers. The independent sailor figure is an appealing one in this form of psychological projection, because he is clearly separated from the land of home and mother and he has a reputation for lustful, boastful behavior. His feisty, insolent character on land is set against the background on water of his submission to the ship's authority, an apparent metaphor for parental control.

An additional implication of the sailor figure is its expression of anxieties by pubertal males about being desirable to women at a time when boys expect the opposite sex to be more attracted to older males. Bill's character is appropriately hypersexed as an older and mature sailor, and yet he is unattractive, in the song's projection of adolescent male anxieties. The female is always young, pretty, and homebound; as a domestic figure, she is commanded by Bill to do his bidding rather than dictating the terms of a relationship by courtship and marriage. She is the object of his affections, but also a epitomization of his submissive self as a feminized, infantilized character who needs to be symbolically vanquished.

Adolescent males hearing that they are supposed to keep their privates in their pants as they mature revel folklorically in Bollocky Bill's propensity for defiantly brandishing his genitals like a penetrative weapon. He will not be restrained by doors, walls, parents, or authorities.

With "Barnacle Bill the Sailor" pervading collegiate and sporting contexts, one may question whether it serves seafarers any longer. I have found that it does, and the contexts for its enactment suggest some different symbols at play as a sailors' ballad. The commercial version of the song by Frank Luther and Carson Robison is included in the official *Navy Song Book* issued by the United States Department of the Navy, but this reference is more of a reminder of saltier folk versions than a master text for sailors (Bureau of Naval Personnel 1958: song 25). The song is frequently part of both formal and informal celebrations on ship.

Postcard featuring the musical band "Barnacle Bill and His Sailors," composed of seamen, c. 1960 (author's collection).

A formal context is known by the less than noble title of "mess night" or "dining-in." It is a military ceremony often traced to British origins in Admiral Horatio Nelson's heyday of the late eighteenth century and actively observed still in the US Navy. The ceremony originally took the form of lavish feasts celebrating military victories at which officers dined together with common sailors. It is now a formal assembly that features a fancy banquet followed by folk entertainments. The mess night meal often includes the traditional manly entree of roast beef and generous supplies of wine. In a ceremonial part of the meal, tables are cleared and selected speakers give a round of tributary toasts. Mess dinner today may commemorate a special event such as the anniversary of the battle of Trafalgar or the battle of Midway, or crossing of the equator or international date line. After the conclusion of the meal and toasts, and sometimes the distribution of cigars (and the designation of a "smoking lamp" that is lighted), the event frequently features a humorous skit, game-playing (known as "wardroom games" often involving the performance of embarrassing stunts), and group singing. The songs celebrate sailor identity and heritage with naval hymns and sea chanties, but also include risque songs representing manly toughness and, it appears, fidelity to the sea rather than to sweethearts and mother onshore. The sixteen songs catalogued by Charles J. Gibowicz in *Mess Night Traditions* (2007) include, for example, "Drunken Sailor," "There Are No Navy Pilots Down in Hell," "Bell Bottom Trousers," and "Barnacle Bill the Sailor" (2007: 219–20).

"Barnacle Bill" is not the only dialogue song at mess nights. Another favorite is "Reuben and Rachel" found in many variations (composition credited to Harry Birch, 1871) in which Rachel reflects in the opening about the changes that occur to men "far beyond the Northern Sea":

> Reuben, Reuben, I've been thinking
> What a queer world this would be
> If the men were all transported
> Far beyond the Northern Sea.

Reuben's reply, sung by the men in unison, is:

> Rachel, Rachel, I've been thinking
> If we went beyond the seas
> All the girls would follow after
> Like a swarm of honey bees.

But the women respond that the men are not wanted back on land:

> Reuben, Reuben, I've been thinking
> Life would be so easy then
> What a lovely world this would be
> If there were no tiresome men.

(Gibowicz 2007: 218–19).

The song sets up the dialogue in versions of "Barnacle Bill" sung at mess night dinners in which the maiden asks for marriage that will domesticate the sailor, or "tie him down." The response from Bill is that he has a woman in every port. "I courts 'em all but marries none," Bill boasts. The song at mess night dinners usually concludes then with "Tonight I'm sailing from the shore."

"Barnacle Bill" is especially prevalent at "Neptune's Ball," often held after equator crossings. Encouraging the dialogue song is cross-dressing that occurs in which men dressed as women take the maiden's parts. These performances, overseen by "Neptune's Court" ruled by King Neptune, involve master and "old man" of the raging main, and other unsavory characters such as Davy Jones, Royal Executioner, Royal Doctor, Royal Scribe, and pirate figures.

The singers mock femininity and uphold the sailor's life as independent of all other identities, on land or in the military. The bearded Neptune is presented as the god of the deep and he comes on board with a phallic trident (see Dundes 2008: 70).

The play frame forms out of the perception that the equator signals a ritual reversal, from obedient sailor to surly pirate, as well as men to women. Sailors refer to the ceremony as "crossing the line" referring literally to moving across the o degrees latitude. Figuratively, lines of decorum are crossed in response to the belief that the equator is far away and lonely. The ceremony normally occurs at a location out of sight of land; Neptune's domain is one that is completely watery. Seamen crossing the equator for the first time have an initiation to endure in which they transform from lowly, slimy pollywogs to hardened shellbacks.

As part of the initiation, they may be ordered to sing "Barnacle Bill." It becomes a shellback anthem. An important part of the ceremony is the initiate's dunking in a tank after being forced to crawl like an infant through a long tube filled with garbage. After emerging from this ritual immersion, he is linked to the ship by being showered or sprayed with water. The ritual represents a symbolic transformation by which water is no longer the nurturing womb of the mother on land and instead epitomizes entrance into a dangerous, "raging" realm of the vast, deep sea. This domain is rendered masculine by a Neptune as supreme deity. Tribute is given to him for his command of the deep and his rule over his feminine queen and an abundance of mermaids.

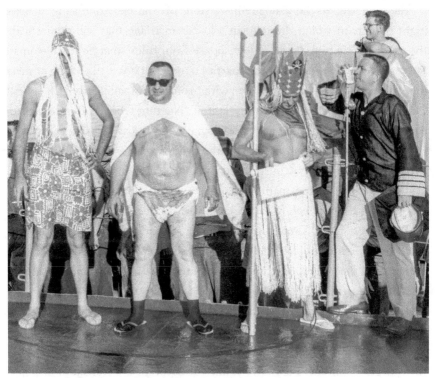

Ceremony for crossing equator on board a United States ship, February 2, 1965. From left to right: Royal Queen; royal Baby (with soiled diapers); King Neptune; Royal Navigator (author's collection).

Barnacle Bill in the singular domain of the sea is "a really nasty character, gross and vicious, without respect for woman, child or society," according to Anthony Hopkins, who has documented the song among Canadian servicemen. He points out that "These are, however, useful qualities for a man to have if he wants to convince himself that he doesn't mind danger, that he's rough and tough and more than a match for anything—civilized or savage—that might trap him into being less brave, less callous, less confident than he needs to be to survive" (Hopkins 1979: 151).

As a ballad, "Barnacle Bill" dramatizes a narrative of separation. Instead of bemoaning his isolation from people and ground beneath his feet, Bill is one with the danger and defiance of the sea. He turns his liability on land of his crudeness into a characteristic of being out on the waters. It is important that they are "open" waters of the ocean, for they represent a total environment in which men are dominant.

In contrast, a number of legends refer to Barnacle Bill "tied down" in lakes inland. For example, the folklore archives at the University of Oregon are filled with accounts of "Barnacle Bill legends" in Lake Wakoma. Sea anemones accumulated on pilings appear to form the outline of a body, which is explained this way: "Supposedly Barnacle Bill had a fight with his wife, and she tied him there" (Randall V. Mills Archives 1972). Out on the ocean, Bill has a woman in every port to represent his inability to be domesticated and implicitly a tie to his mother. He will not be constrained by societal authority either and he demonstrates his power not just by muscular strength but also by his male generative glands.

Occasionally, singers have characterized Bill as a pilot or cowboy, but he keeps coming back as a sailor because that role provides the most separation from the man's feminine qualities and maternal ties. Sailors are aware that on ship they take on feminine roles of cleaning, sewing, and cooking, and appear to compensate with the aid of folkloric performances that emphasize their hyper-sexuality to express hyper-masculinity. In this presentation of themselves, they often confront perceptions of them as feminine or repressed, especially in light of a prominent historic ballad theme of women who disguise themselves as sailors (although the ruse is narratively explained by the role of the females as juvenile "cabin boys" who are discovered when they become pregnant on shipboard) (Frank 2010: 185–94; Greenhill 2003; Palmer 1986: 202–3). In line with this perception, contemporary sailors voice the opinion that they are more submissive to hierarchical command than other services. Former Navy man Alan Dundes notes that "They are told when and what to eat, when to go to bed, what to wear, and just about when to urinate and defecate" (Dundes 2007: 380). He suggests that projections in folklore occur in this repressive environment involving erotic fantasies as signs of resistance to domination by exhibiting subordination of others, particularly feminine characters. Further, they are subject to the suspicion of homosexual intimacy because of living in close quarters with men for long periods (see Zeeland 1995). In psychological as well as popular culture chronicles, they tend to be dominated by mothers. In folklore, they often run away to the sea to separate from them.

EXPLAINING BARNACLE BILL AND HIS MATES

"Barnacle Bill," I propose, is more than bawdy tomfoolery. Its sexual humor may in fact be enacted to mask anxieties of gender identity and social power relationships in situations where men are isolated or put into a submissive state. Particularly in the master-servant relationship of the ship in which ties are symbolically cut off from land, mother, and femininity, the song for sailors has a dramatic narrative to render about separation from the domestication of home and family. To others, it has held appeal as a masculine fantasy about fulfilling sexual desire and in changing times, a feminist commentary on sexual power.

The keys to the meaning are provided by the standard opening of "Who's that knocking at my door?," which suggests a border between the familiar land and the strange water from whence sailors come. The sailor is the stranger, the fearsome intruder who does not fit in, socially or sexually. He is barnacled socially as a seaman who has spent years at his trade and has become inextricably socialized into a singular domain. He is also bollocky physically to represent the consequences of being in an all-male domain. His hyper-masculinity stands out and the question arises whether it is an affront or asset. Second, almost inevitably Bill announces himself as "me from across the sea" indicating that home is on the waters. He is defined not by where he grew up but by where he dwells. That watery place is uncertain because it appears indefinable as well as remote. The location is also dangerous and raises doubts about the kind of people who would choose that life.

Barnacle Bill as a modern narrative since industrialization and now into the cyber-age uses the sailor character to express a hyper-masculine fantasy in the context of an increasingly feminized society. The play frames that allow its performance refer to practices that appear out of place: rugby playing in sports, camp during school years, intellectual college experience in adulthood, and seafaring in a landed, corporate age. The song can be performed to show how ridiculous the fantasy of hyper-masculinity is or how pressing is the context of feminization. In approval for its humor and transgression, audiences, particularly when they participate in the song's performance, contribute to the accumulation of symbolic capital for men. Despite John Ashton's pronouncement in 1891 that sailor balladry is dead and gone, the folk songs of the sea still have an imaginative hold in male maturation, and arguably, on the social construction of gender. Of those songs, Barnacle Bill is in my estimation the most persistent and pervasive. The sailor in the song is rhetorically presented not as a regionally limited occupational character but a device to explore the maturing self. The sailor epitomizes the symbolic separation of water and land into categories of masculine and feminine, independence and domestication, and old age and youth.

The continuity of "Barnacle Bill" with the "sailor ballads of old" is well expressed by Ashton when he claims that the sailor "in his Love Songs, he, certainly, put a full value on himself. Then—according to the nautical poet— maidens of high degree, and rich matrons, thought themselves all but unworthy of the hand of an A. B., and many were the matrimonial prizes, according to Song, that fell to Jack's share—the young ladies going absolutely wild after him—defying their parents, nay, even the elements themselves, and stripping themselves of all maidenly reserve, in order to unite themselves to, or even to be in the same ship with, the object of their passion." (1891: 2)

The dramatic tension in old and new songs is the absence of sailors from land out on the open waters, which raises questions both about their ties to land and loved ones left home, and their relationships to other sailors as people of the sea. The veil of humor in the play frame of the song allows these troubling questions to be raised and narrated through symbolic projections. Sailors may no longer sing for work, but they nonetheless invoke sailors' musical heritage as markers of identity with suggestions of a collective personality. That identity is even more strained than before because venturing out into the seven seas does not appear in modernity to be economically or politically central. Singing for sailors on ritual occasions often addresses anxieties about their choice of careers and the sacrifices they have made to be isolated on the ocean.

Sailors I have interviewed typically express high satisfaction in their work and the opportunities to travel to exotic sites, but recognize that being away for long stretches of time in environments that could not be called "homey" appears odd to landlubbers. In the lore of their contemporary songs, they declare their superiority over land, authority, and women. They turn an endeavor that landlubbers belittle into a badge of distinction—a sign of toughness signifying social dominance. The songs also emphasize that they are out of place on land; they are most at home in the sea.

I recognize a difference in the irreverent lot of "Barnacle Bill" from the classic set of naval ballads in Ashton's compendium. Neither meant for forecastle or wardroom, these modernized ballads are stripped of sentiment and located in fantasy (and folklore) with their bawdiness for various festive gatherings. For seamen, they fulfill ritual roles in ceremonies that mark life as a sailor. Rather than, as Ashton intimated, sailors feeling the love in song from ashore, however, the anti-sentimental ballads show a projective inversion involving the low reputation of sailors and their expressive culture: instead of conveying through sexuality and violence "they [land, society, women] hate me." The lore broadcasts the message, "I hate them."

Further, in lieu of showing their submission in a severe hierarchical situation on ship, the songs proclaim the sailors' independence and social dominance. For others in high-context settings such as rugby teams, college fraternities, and summer camps, the ballads appropriate the sailor's defiance and inversion of submission in song to emblematize anxieties of separation from femininity and infantalization associated with urbanized mass culture. If not necessarily "odorous of the sea," as Ashton recalled of the early nineteenth-century variety of sailor songs, the newer iteration of parodic seamen's ballads nonetheless uses the open waters to symbolize the estrangement of men.

REFERENCES

Abrahams, Roger D. 1963. "Some Jump-Rope Rimes from Texas." *Southern Folklore Quarterly* 27: 196–213.

Anonymous. 1974. "Barnacle Bill the Sailor." Typescript. Indiana State University Folklore Archives.

A. P. H. 1920. "The Barnacle (A Sort of Sea Shanty)." *Punch* 159 (December 8): 455.

Ashton, John, ed. 1891. *Real Sailor-Songs*. London: Leadenhall Press.

Baker, Ronald L., and Simon J. Bronner. 2005. "'Letting Out Jack': Sex and Aggression in Manly Recitations." In *Manly Traditions: The Folk Roots of American Masculinities*, ed. Simon J. Bronner, 315–50. Bloomington: Indiana University Press.

Baring-Gould, S., and Cecil J. Sharp. 1907. *English Folk-Songs for Schools*. London: J. Curwen & Sons.

Baskerville, Charles Read. 1921. "English Songs of the Night Visit." *Publications of the Modern Language Association* 36: 565–614.

Beck, Horace P. 1949. "Review of *American Sea Songs and Chanteys from the Days of Iron Men and Wooden Ships* Edited by Frank Shay." *Journal of American Folklore* 62: 332–33.

Bennett, Harold, comp. 2000. *Bawdy Ballads & Dirty Ditties of the Wartime R.A.F.* Bognor Regis, UK: Woodfield Publishing.

Boyes, Marcia Edwards. 1936. *The Legend of Yerba Buena Island*. Berkeley, California: Professional Press.

Brewster, Paul G., ed. 1940. *Ballads and Songs of Indiana*. Bloomington: Indiana University Publications.

Broadwood, Lucy E. 1928. "Early Chanty-Singing and Ship-Music." *Journal of the Folk-Song Society* 8: 55–60.

Bronner, Simon J. 1987. *Old-Time Music Makers of New York State*. Syracuse: Syracuse University Press.

_____. 1988. *American Children's Folklore*. Little Rock: August House.

_____. 2006. *Crossing the Line: Violence, Play, and Drama in Naval Equator Traditions*. Amsterdam: Amsterdam University Press.

Brophy, John, and Eric Partridge. 1931. *Songs and Slang of the British Soldier: 1914–1918*. London: Scholartis Press.

Buntline, Ned. 1873a. "Barnacle Bill; Or, the Hut on Devil's Peak." *New York Weekly*, July 28, pp. 1–2.

_____. 1873b. "Barnacle Bill; Or, the Hut on Devil's Peak." *New York Weekly*, August 4, pp. 1–2.

_____. 1881. *Buffalo Bill: The King of Border Men*. New York: J.S. Ogilvie.

Bureau of Naval Personnel, Special Services Division, Music Branch. 1958. *Navy Song Book*. Washington, D.C.: Department of the Navy.

Burton, Roger V., and John W. M. Whiting. 1961. "The Absent Father and Cross-Sex Identity." *Merrill-Palmer Quarterly of Behavior and Development* 7: 85–95.

Cattermole-Tally, Frances. 1987–88. "The *Tagelied* and Other Dawn Songs: The Parting of Lovers, Living and Dead." 11–12: 15–35.

"Cinema: The New Pictures." 1928. *Time* (March 5). time.com/time/magazine/article/0,9171,880965–1.html. Accessed June 29, 2010.

Colcord, Joanna C. 1964. *Songs of American Sailormen*. New York: Oak Archives.

Cray, Ed. 1992. *The Erotic Muse: American Bawdy Songs*. Urbana: University of Illinois Press.

Dorson, Richard M. 1957. "Collecting Folklore in Jonesport, Maine." *Proceedings of the American Philosophical Society* 101: 270–89.

Dundes, Alan. 2007a. "How Indic Parallels to the Ballad of the 'Walled-Up Wife' Reveal the Pitfalls of Parochial Nationalistic Folkloristics." In *The Meaning of Folklore: The Analytical Essays of Alan Dundes*, ed. Simon J. Bronner, 107–22. Logan: Utah State Univ.Press.

_____. 2007b. "The Kushmaker." In *The Meaning of Folklore: The Analytical Essays of Alan Dundes*, ed. Simon J. Bronner, 375–81. Logan: Utah State University Press.

_____. 2008. *Bloody Mary in the Mirror: Essays in Psychoanalytic Folkloristics*. Jackson: University Press of Mississippi.

Davids, C.A. 1980. *Watlijdt den zeeman al verdriet: Het Nederlandse zeemanslied in de zeiltijd (1600–1900)*. The Hague: Martinus Nijhoff.

Davis, Arthur Kyle, Jr. 1928. "Some Problems of Ballad Publication." *Musical Quarterly* 14: 283–96.

Flanders, Helen Hartness, and George Brown, eds. 1931. *Vermont Folk-Songs & Ballads*. Brattleboro: Stephen Daye Press.

Fowke, Edith. 1970. *Lumbering Songs from the Northern Woods*. Austin: University of Texas Press.

Frank, Stuart M. 1996. *Ooh, You New York Girls! The Urban Pastorale in Ballads and Songs about Sailors Ashore in the Big City*. Sharon, Massachusetts: Kendall Whaling Museum.

_____. 2010. *Jolly Sailors Bold: Ballads and Songs of the American Sailor*. East Windsor, New Jersey: Camsco Music.

Gentleman About Town, A. 1927. *Immortalia: An Anthology of American Ballads, Sailors' Songs, Cowboy Songs, College Songs, Parodies, Limericks, and Other Humorous Verses and Doggerel Now for the First Time Brought Together in Book Form*. Privately Printed.

Fuld, James J. 1985. *The Book of World-Famous Music: Classical, Popular and Folk*, 3rd ed. New York: Dover.

Gibowicz, Charles J. 2002. *Mess Night Traditions*. Bloomington, Indiana: AuthorHouse.

Gilchrist, Annie G. 1924a. "Dance Tunes." *Journal of the Folk-Song Society* 7: 171–74.

_____. 1924b. "Good-Night and Parting Songs: In Relation to the Night Visit and the 'Aubade' or Dawn Song; With Manx Examples." *Journal of the Folk-Song Society* 7: 184–94.

Gilchrist, Annie G., and Lucy E. Broadwood. 1924. "Songs of Courtship." *Journal of the Folk-Song Society* 7: 135–47.

Gould, S. Baring, and Cecil J. Sharp. 1907. *English Folk-Songs for Schools*. London: J. Curwen & Sons.

Green, Douglas. 1971. "From Broadside Ballad to 'The Nashville Sound': The Evolution of 'A Pretty Fair Maiden in the Garden.'" *Journal of Country Music* 2: 10–17.

Greenhill, Pauline. 2003. "'Places She Knew Very Well': The Symbolic Economy of Women's Travels in Traditional Newfoundland Ballads." In *The Flowering Thorn: International Ballad Studies*, ed. Thomas A. McKean, 55–66. Logan: Utah State University Press.

Grønseth, Erik, and Per Olav Tiller. 1957. "The Impact of Father Absence in Sailor Families upon the Personality Structure and Social Adjustment of Adult Sailor Sons." *Studies of the Family* 2: 97–114.

Halliwell, James Orchard. 1841. *Early Naval Ballads of England*. London: Percy Society.

Halyard, Ned. 1849. *Sea Songs, Tales, Etc.* London: Palmer & Hoby.

Hand, Wayland D. 1986. "Introduction." In *The Ballad and the Scholars: Approaches to Ballad Study* by D.K. Wilgus and Barre Toelken, vii–xi. Los Angeles: William Andrews Clark Memorial Library, University of California.

Hansen, Wm. F. 1976. "The Story of the Sailor Who Went Inland." In *Folklore Today: A Festschrift for Richard M. Dorson*, ed. Linda Dégh, Henry Glassie, and Felix J. Oinas, 221–30. Bloomington: Research Center for Language and Semiotic Studies, Indiana University.

Harlow, Frederick Pease. 2004 [1962]. *Chanteying Aboard American Ships*. Mystic, Connecticut: Mystic Seaport.

Henderson, Hamish. 1947. *Ballads of World War II*. Glasgow: Lili Marleen Club.

Hoffmann, Frank. 1973. *Analytical Survey of Anglo-American Traditional Erotica*. Bowling Green, Ohio: Bowling Green State University Popular Press.

Hopkins, Anthony. 1979. *Songs from the Front & Rear: Canadian Servicemen's Songs of the Second World War*. Edmonton: Hurtig Publishers.

"Horrible Deeds of a Wrecker." 1871. *St. Albans Messenger* (St. Albans, VT), January 6, p. 9.

Hotten, John Camden, ed. 1913. *The Slang Dictionary: Etymological, Historical and Anecdotal*. London: Chatto & Windus.

Hugill, Stan. 1961. *Shanties from the Seven Seas: Shipboard Work-Songs and Songs Used as Work-Songs from the Great Days of Sail*. London: Routledge & Kegan Pual.

Jewett, Sophie. 1913. *Folk-Ballads of Southern Europe*. New York: G.P. Putnam's Sons.

Johnson, James, and William Stenhouse. 1803. *The Scots Musical Museum*, 4 vols. Edinburgh: William Blackwood and Sons.

Johnson, John Henry, ed. 1935. *Bawdy Ballads and Lusty Lyrics*. Indianapolis: M. Droke.

Kryptádia: Recueil de documents pour servir à l'étude des traditions populaires, vol. 2. 1884. Heilbronn: Henninger Frères.

Kryptádia: Recueil de documents pour servir à l'étude des traditions populaires, vol. 5. 1898. Paris: H. Welter.

Laws, Malcolm G., Jr. 1964. *Native American Balladry: A Descriptive Study and a Bibliographical Syllabus*. Philadelphia: American Folklore Society.

Legman, G. 1964. *The Horn Book: Studies in Erotic Folklore and Bibliography*. New Hyde Park, New York: University Books.

Linton, E.R., comp. 1965. *The Dirty Song Book: American Bawdy Songs*. Los Angeles: Medco Books.

Lomax, Alan. 1960. *The Folk Songs of North America*. New York: Doubleday.

Lyle, E. B. Lyle, ed. 1975. *Andrew Crawfurd's Collection of Ballads and Songs*, Vol. 1. Edinburgh: Scottish Text Society.

Lynn, Frank. 1963. *Songs for Swingin' Housemothers*. New York: Oak.

Lyra Ebriosa: Being Certain Narrative Ballads of a Vulgar or Popular Character and Illustrative of the Manners of the Times. 1933. Privately Printed.

Martinengo-Cesaresco, Countess Evelyn. 1886. *Essays in the Study of Folk-Songs*. London: George Redway.

Meertens Instituut. 2010. "Broadside Ballads: A Collection of the Meertens Instituut, the Koninklijke Bibliotheek." http://www.geheugenvannederland.nl/?/en/collecties/straatliederen. Accessed June 29, 2010.

Monaghan, Jay. 1951. *The Great Rascal: The Life and Adventures of Ned Buntline*. New York: Bonanza Books.

Morgan, Douglas. 2002. *What Do You Do with a Drunken Sailor?* Pomfret, Connecticut: Swordsmith.

Mullen, Patrick B. 1969. "The Function of Magic Folk Belief among Texas Coastal Fishermen." *Journal of American Folklore* 82: 214–25.

Nemec, David. 2004. *The Beer and Whiskey League: the Illustrated History of the American Association—Baseball's Renegade Major League*. Guildford, Connecticut: Lyons Press.

Newell, William Wells. 1883. *Games and Songs of American Children*. New York: Harper & Bros.

Opie, Iona, and Peter, eds. 1997. *The Oxford Dictionary of Nursery Rhymes*. Oxford, England: Oxford University Press.

Owens, William A. 1950. *Texas Folk Songs*. Austin: Texas Folklore Society.

Page, Martin, ed. 1975. *The Bawdy Songs & Ballads of World War II: Kiss Me Goodnight, Sergeant Major*. London: Granada.

Palmer, Roy, ed. 1986. *The Oxford Book of Sea Songs*. Oxford, England: Oxford Univ. Press.

Partridge, Eric. 1970. *A Dictionary of Slang and Unconventional English*. New York: Macmillan.

Patrick, John. 2006. "Barnacle Bill the Sailor." *DrinkingSongs.net* www.csufresno.edu/folklore/drinkingsongs/html/categorized-by-song/with-music/b/bollochy-bill-the-sailor.htm. Accessed December 10, 2010.

Poggie, John J, Jr.; Richard B. Pollnac; Carl Gersuny. 1976. "Risk as a Basis for Taboos Among Fishermen in Southern New England." *Journal for the Scientific Study of Religion* 15: 257–62.

Pyles, Thomas. 1949. "Innocuous Linguistic Indecorum: A Semantic Byway." *Modern Language Notes* 64: 1–8.

Randall V. Mills Archives of Northwest Folklore. 1972. "Camp Legend-Barnacle Bill." Typescript.

Randolph, Vance. 1992. *"Unprintable" Ozark Folksongs and Folklore*, 2 Vols. ed. G. Legman. Fayetteville: University of Arkansas Press.

Read, Allen Walker. 1949. "The Status of Bollix." *American Speech* 24: 153–54.

Rennick, Robert M. 1959. "The Disguised Lover Theme and the Ballad." *Southern Folklore Quarterly* 23: 215–32.

———. 1963. "The Pretty Fair Maid in the Garden." *Southern Folklore Quarterly* 27: 229–46.

Renwick, Roger deV. 1985. "On the Interpretation of Folk Poetry." In *Narrative Folksong: New Directions. Essays in Appreciation of W. Edson Richmond*, ed. Carol L. Edwards and Kathleen E. B. Manley, 401–34. Boulder, Colorado: Westview Press.

Reuss, Richard. 1965. "An Annotated Field Collection of Songs from the American College Student Oral Tradition." Ph.D. dissertation, Indiana University.

Richmond, W. Edson. 1989. *Ballad Scholarship: An Annotated Bibliography*. New York: Garland.

Rugby Songs. 2007. rugbysongs.net/rugbysng.pdf. Accessed June 29, 2010.

Sailor Boy and Songs. 1852. Concord, New Hampshire: Rufus Merrill.

Sauls, Beth. 1981. "Barnacle Bill the Sailor." Typescript. University of California, Berkeley, Folklore Archives.

Saunders, William. 1928. "Sailor Songs and Songs of the Sea." *Musical Quarterly* 14: 339–57.

"Seal-Fishery Disasters and the 'Times's' Story, The." 1872. *Evening Post* (New York, NY), July 9.

Shay, Frank. 1961. *My Pious Friends and Drunken Companions AND More Pious Friends and Drunken Companions*. New York: Dover.

———. 1991. *An American Sailor's Treasury: Sea Songs, Chanteys, Legends, and Lore*. New York: Smithmark.

Shoolbraid, Murray, ed. 2010. *The High-Kilted Muse: Peter Buchan and His Secret Songs of Silence*. Jackson: University Press of Mississippi.

Smith, Laura Alexandrine. 1888. *The Music of the Waters: A Collection of the Sailors' Chanties, or Working Songs of the Sea, of All Maritime Nations. Boatmen's, Fishermen's, and Rowing Songs, and Water Legends*. London: Kegan Paul, Trench & Co.

Speaight, George, ed. 1975. *Bawdy Songs of the Early Music Hall*. Newton Abbot: David & Charles.

Spring, Ian. 1988. "Why Did 'the Bridegroom Greet'?" *Folk Music Journal* 5: 469–81.

Thompson, Harold W., ed. 2009 [1958]. *A Pioneer Songster: Texts from the Stevens-Douglass Manuscript of Western New York, 1841–1856*. Ithaca: Cornell University Press.

Toelken, Barre. 1995. *Morning Dew and Roses: Nuance, Metaphor, and Meaning in Folksongs*. Urbana: University of Illinois Press.

Visweswaran, Kamala. 1981. "Buffalo Bill the Sailor." Musical Transcription. University of California, Berkeley, Folklore Archives.

Wilgus, D.K. 1959. *Anglo-American Folksong Scholarship Since 1898*. New Brunswick, New Jersey: Rutgers University Press.

"Wrecker, A." 1871. *Alexandria Gazette* (Alexandria, VA), November 21, p. 1.

Zeeland, Steven. 1995. *Sailors and Sexual Identity: Crossing the Line Between "Straight" and "Gay" in the U.S. Navy*. Binghamton, New York: Haworth Press.

Simon J. Bronner is Distinguished Professor of American Studies and Folklore and chair of the American Studies Program at the Pennsylvania State University, Harrisburg. He has also taught at Harvard University, Dickinson College, University of California at Davis, Osaka University (Japan), and Leiden University (Netherlands). He is the author and editor of over 35 books on folklore and cultural history, including recently *Folklore: The Basics* (Routledge, 2017), *Youth Cultures in America* (Greenwood, 2016), Campus Traditions (University Press of Mississippi, 2012), *Explaining Traditions* (University Press of Kentucky 2011), *Encyclopedia of American Folklife* (4 vols., M.E. Sharpe, 2006), *Crossing the Line* (Amsterdam University Press, 2006), and Manly Traditions (Indiana University Press, 2005). His *Old-Time Music Makers of New York State* (Syracuse University Press, 1987) won the John Ben Snow Foundation Prize and the Award of Merit from the Regional Council of Historical Societies. He has received numerous other awards for his scholarship and teaching, including the Kenneth Goldstein Award for Lifetime Academic Leadership, Peter and Iona Opie Award for children's folklore, the Wayland D. Hand Prize for folklore and history from the American Folklore Society, Mary Turpie Prize from the American Studies Association, and the Doctoral Teaching Award from the Northeastern Association of Graduate Schools. He has served as President of the Fellows of the American Folklore Society, Western States Folklore Society, and the Middle Atlantic Folklife Association. He has received fellowships from the National Endowment for the Humanities, Rockefeller Foundation, McCormick Foundation, and National Endowment for the Arts for his research.

Lightning Source UK Ltd.
Milton Keynes UK
UKHW022247041222
413345UK00012B/1671

9 781935 243830